UNBOUND
Out of the Darkness of Mental Illness

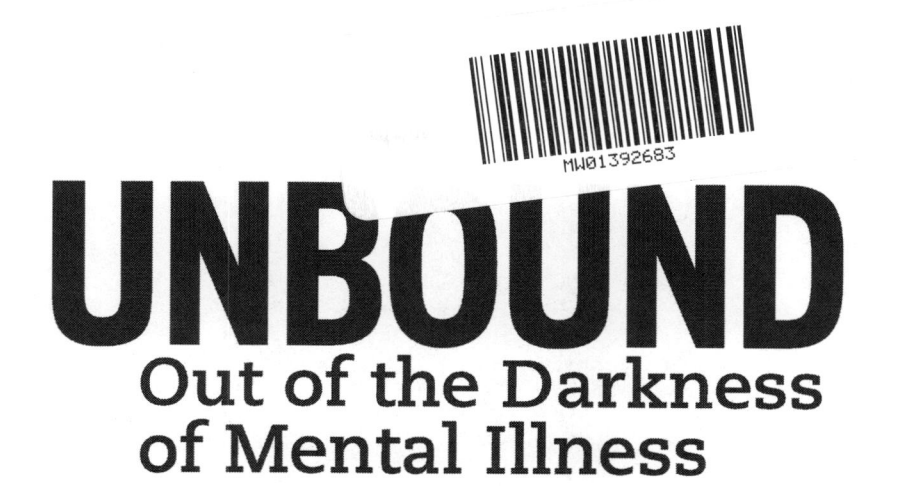

KELLY JADON

INTO THE
DEEP
BOOKS

Unbound
Out of the Darkness of Mental Illness

Copyright © 2018 Kelly Jadon

Printed in the United States of America

ISBN: 978-0-9903751-4-2

All rights reserved. No part of this publication may be reproduced, stored in a retrieval system, or transmitted in way form or by any means—for example, electronic, photocopy, recording—without the prior written permission of the author, except as provided by United States of America copyright law and indicated by the author.

Unless otherwise indicated, all Scripture quotations are from are from the New American Standard Bible.

For more information about this author's book and writing, please visit: www.kellyjadon.com

All rights reserved.

INTO THE
DEEP
B O O K S

Acknowledgements

Special thanks to Kathy Curtis, my typesetter; Brenda Haun, my cover artist on whom I rely for publishing assistance; Dr. Helena Mariades, who never gave up on me; my enduring and loving husband Rafat; my children whom I love dearly; Dr. Dennis Garn, former English Literature professor of Spring Arbor University who brought out my love of words in poetry; Dr. Robert Verno, Pastor of West Shore Brethren in Christ, who baptized me; friends some here and others gone to Heaven who touched my life for the better—*thank you.*

Unbound is dedicated to Lord Jesus. This book is possible because of the unfailing love of God, Who called me while I was yet in my mother's womb and made the way out of darkness when I could see no way out. Ten percent of the proceeds of *Unbound's* sales will be returned to God through His church.

"For I am convinced that neither death nor life, neither angels nor demons, neither the present nor the future, nor any powers, neither height nor depth, nor anything else in all creation, will be able to separate us from the love of God that is in Christ Jesus our Lord." *(Romans 8:38-39)*

table of contents

introduction **15**
testimony 16
my story 17

back story **22**
first thoughts 23
robbed 24
truth 25
the swamp 26
loneliness 26
by mother's hands 27
her hands 27
why? 29
can i? 29
mom 30
traces of grace 31
not all 31
reality and fantasy 32
scars 34
reckless 35
the curse 36
freemason curse 36
the rhubarb 39
all things 39
snow pile 40
spirits enter 43

the spot *45*
false shame *46*
the talk *47*
boundaries *48*

interlude **49**
reflection at 19 .... *50*
believer *52*
florida *53*

deeper **54**
dad *55*
it is not *56*
how? *56*
He says *57*
nicely nurse *58*
door opening *59*
saul's search *59*
death *60*
occult *61*
attacks *66*
doors *67*
death *68*
to live *68*

back doors **70**
deceit *71*
back doors *73*
sound mind *75*

back door: meditation **76**
entrance *77*
meditate *78*
yoga *79*
heart *80*
corpse *81*
giving over *82*

table of contents

meditation's roots *83*
kundalini *84*
transcendentalism *86*
portals *87*
chakras *89*
the 7 .... *91*
truth? *98*
symbols *101*
kalki *103*
reincarnation *105*

deep things *107*
deep things *108*
the occult *110*
inside the church *113*
spirits *117*
roulette *119*
the book *121*
the stone *124*
my friend *125*
the heart *127*
abyss *129*
readings *130*
cassadega *140*
aliens *144*

healing *146*
the prescription *147*
edgar cayce *150*
infusion *155*
energy *156*
unity *158*
out! *160*

war *161*
a military *162*
fleshly armies *167*

isolation *172*
the shield *177*
the sword *180*
together *183*
death's door *186*
no surrender *188*
casting out *190*
break it *191*
after *192*

to God **193**
i ran *194*
melt down *195*
paper dolls *196*
paranoia *199*
struggle for self *200*
the house *201*
the place *203*
the precipice *205*
what happened *205*
the prophet *207*
the pull *208*
tabebuia tree *209*
the trial *211*
after the trial *212*
voices *213*
who am i? *214*

pulled out **215**
first strike: a call to God *216*
first nights *217*
deceiver *218*
so simple *219*
last glance *221*
territory *223*
the basement *224*

the bridge......226
the counselor......228
the heart......229
my Anchor......230
the husband......231
the osprey......232

finding self......**234**
a key......235
memories......235
bone-tired......236
strength......236
each day......237
new days......238
false shame......239
despised......240
instead......241
all things......241
lost time......243
one word......245
the wall......246
pony......247
rocks......248
sin......250
the dig......252
the door......254
grape vine......256

cycling down......**258**
green cross dream......259
privacy......262
selah......263
transitions......264
He takes......266
the meat......268
the covenant: a delusion......270

standing: satan uses me..*274*
now they know *275*
new covenant...*276*

transition..**278**
transition *279*
strategic..*280*
lowly...*281*
quiet strength..*282*
word curse...*283*
revenge not *284*
promised *285*
burdens lifted..*286*

ready to use my own name..**287**
birthing *288*
the trigger..*290*
misunderstood *291*
you wish to die? *293*

About the Author..**297**

Lord, make my life a miracle…..

introduction

testimony

"i've come to tell you a story.
there's a switchblade
in the indian river
with my name
and my blood on it.
do you want to listen?"

introduction

my story

this is my story
of God's power
over
death, despair
mental illness
and how it's linked with
demonization
and its symptoms, causes
generational iniquity
generational curses
strongholds

disassociation
OCD
paranoia
post traumatic stress
schizo-affective disorder
co-dependency
depression
manic
anxiety
hallucinations
major depression
thoughts of suicide

anger
bitterness
shame
guilt
rejection

hiding
running away
broken boundaries
self-punishing

perfectionism
driven
weakness

dad's death
hospice
where attacks worsened

drawn to death
the dying
raymond moody

inviting in the enemy
the occult
visualization
gongs
self-hypnosis
portals
meditation
kabbala
unity "church"

the paranormal
synchronicity
light workers
spiritualism
word curses
reiki
yoga
aura
tarot cards

demonic movement
energy roving
on/off
on/off
lights

introduction

music
words in ears

darkness opened doors
a deepening desire of the flesh
to more darkness—

cassadega
        a spirit prayed in
moving of my spirit
reincarnation
edgar cayce
santeria
voodoo
askashic and psychic readers
a written horoscope
                proclaiming my death

attacks
physical:
        car crash, depression, snake, near drowning, near plane crash, near suicide
        depletion: serotonin, vitamin B12, vitamin D, severe hormone imbalance, anemia, adrenal overload
        genetic inheritance depression, anxiety, seeing things
spiritual:
        impressed visions, impressed dreams, astro-projection
        Words of God twisted, false signs and wonders
the two affected the mental

what happened to me
began before i was born
not my fault
abuse followed

a born-again believer
the enemy played me

over and over
like a guitar
each day strumming the chords
turning me this way, that
creating divisions
between husband and wife
mother and children

each day the enemy
boosted me up
pushing me to a work-led
breakdown
creating me to be
something i was never called
to be
using my gifts, talents
for its own evil purposes
deceived

i was deceived
and thought i followed God

my story
here
that you may know
the thoughts within
the mentally ill,
the demon tricks
devilish devices
to take a life
too early

how he plays
games
mind control
like cat and mouse
good cop—bad cop

introduction

glorying in calling
himself
God the Father
God the Son
God—Holy Spirit
but he is none

what happened to me
happens to others
i consider myself fortunate
but my past is here
in writing
that you might know and understand
how i fell to mental illness
how i went in to the occult
and how i
a woman of no repute
a woman of dust
came out
by the power of God
the power of the Blood
and the power of the Lamb

"You will know the truth, and the truth will make you free."
(John 8:32)

back story

first thoughts

when i was a child
i thought as a child
i innocently believed what i heard
even before i was born

when i was a child
i thought as a child
i was taught as a child
"Jesus Loves Me"
my first song

when i was a child
i thought as a child
hiding His Words
deep in my heart
"Jesus loves me
this i know"

when i became a woman
i put away childish things
but my first song
"Jesus Loves Me"
prepared me
preserved me
til death's door was padlocked
by the Blood of the Lamb

yes Jesus loves me
the Bible tells me so*

*"Jesus Loves Me" by Anna Bartlett Warner, William Batchelder Bradbury

robbed

the child
yet a babe
cried in her crib
hair soft brown
grown long
cried for love, attention
arms to hold her

at the head stood
the doctor
spoon in hand
pushing medicine
into the open mouth
head craned up
exposing neck's gash
ragged oval of deep darkness
pitched black

the way blocked
by the mother
i could not help the babe
her voice cut off
her life time-robbed
harmed

a dream
from the Lord

truth

truth
shall set you free
of dissociation
its roots
crib beginnings—
1964

2009
i cried from my bed
"help me God!"
silently
yet without my voice

He came
crushed enemies
stood me up
supporting
my body
my mind
my crushed spirit
in every way

God hears the cry of the lost lamb
rescues with His rod and staff
as He delivered me
He can save you

> "It is He who reveals the profound and hidden things;
> He knows what is in the darkness." (Daniel 2:22)

the swamp
(first published at *GFT Press*)

a retreat from life
in the swamp
where leeches collect
jarred in peanut butter glass
broken tiles
float to clay's clear bottom
rounded by few cat tails
black garters multiply
siphoning water with forks
eggs hatching by hundreds
a gelatinous mass
frogs' eggs suspend
in quiet waters
a child's camp
alone
for fantasies founded
on quiet's aloneness,
solitude and safety's
sake

loneliness

a lifetime's length
but never truly alone
He never left me
"I will never leave you
nor forsake you"

back story

by mother's hands

beside the railroad tie
clod earth buries
daffodil bulbs
by mother's hands
childhood memories

a childhood
idyllic to eyes which
peep from parted
neighbor
curtains

atop the railroad tie
bluegill lay
awaiting gills' knife
and scales' spoon
by mother's hands

a childhood
which was,
when one does not know
what is missing
by mother's hands

her hands

today her hands
clutch
as a bird's
arthritic
unable to hold
what yesterday held
a fishing pole, a spoon

i give thanks
that she yet moves
breathes
in Him
as i do
her smile wide
on Christmas Eve
piano singing
carols ringing
dementia clinging
her days scrape memory
away
scale by scale

why?

why does my mother's voice
cause me to cringe
as bitterness
in the stomach?

why do my memories of her
say hurt
instead of love?

why can't she be
the mother
i want

the one who listens
the one who helps
the one who cares

Lord,
help me to be
the one she never
was

can i?

can i include this poem?
it is truth
but some truths shall remain silent
as the secrets kept within family

mom

her childhood
worse than mine
more dysfunctional
abuse beyond imagination
fear which comes at night
when children should be asleep
no parent near
no one to hear
the silent cry

she created her own small world
pretending that nothing was wrong
denying all ill will,
all evil,
all illness

my mother
with whom my life began,
i am with her
as hers ends,
yet in denial
relationship healed
hurts forgiven
she was but a little girl
who was a better mother
than her own
miracles still happen

> "Remember the wonders He has done, His miracles."
> (1Chronicles 16:12)

traces of grace

traces of grace remain
a hug, a cuddle, a kiss
a special friend who smiled and gave
to a child
made unafraid

traces of grace remind
a swing, a swim, a whirl
time given for laughter and play
to a child
who loved
sunshine's day

traces of grace recall
a snow, a hill, a sled
piled high
a father led
to a child's day
made best of all

not all

not all was ugly
moments of butterfly
happiness
fluttered by
these i keep in my heart
take them out
examining closely
the good
that God provided

reality and fantasy

as a child
my mind fantasized
that i
as wonder woman
could wear a cape
running across seeded summer's grasses
pretending flight
finding disappointment
with gravity's wings

my world became water
when i dove from upper bunk
into undersea life
where people swim instead of walk
beside octopus, sharks and colossal rays

childhood dreams for coping
copied when caught
in adult's stress:
the reality of mental struggle
—acceptance of
doctor's diagnosis,
like a spider's web
too sticky for escape

though i can wish
the world changed
and all things
made perfect—
a utopia
it is not—
for the child
has grown up

back story

at 54
i am not wonder woman
and i cannot do all things
i am instead
a weak woman
no longer young
no longer strong
the days of bearing a child
have dried up
as parched cracked earth
my body has been herniated
mind fragmented
spirit made poor
but to wholeness
He has glued me
with His Blood
and i can yet do
the work
which He has called me
to do
and this is
enough

"i can do all things through Him who strengthens me."
(Philippians 4:13)

scars

pedals push past summer
mother making wheels whir and whiz
beneath furnished feet for toddler totters
across grainy gravel
past neighbor's lake view drives
with child's cheerful hands
c
  l
    u
     t
     c h
    i
  n
g

a
  r
    o
    u
  n
d

her abdomen
a thought of fear whispers through her mind
dangling dainties
little pigs who should have remained at home
cried, "wee!" "wee!" "wee!"
sprained in blood speckled spokes
shoe shorn, torn in tears upon the grass
now bare born
heels torn, scars worn a lifetime
all for fun
hurried to hospital's emergency
newspaper left
unread

reckless

choices made
cause harm
marks remaining
last a lifetime
yet heart healed
forgiven

> "Whenever you stand praying, forgive, if you have anything against anyone, so that your Father who is in heaven will also forgive you your transgressions." (Mark 11:25)

the curse

note to self
        stop worrying about life's experiences, their experientialness notwithstanding turnabout turbinado tornadoes —life's storms leave me stumbling, stuttering, stretched as upon mind's rack—pulled in directions that were non-existent—pulled like a rubber band is stretched—tight, taut, but not snapped, notwithstanding all others. this is resistance—like a white rose in nazi giermany, against evil without incarnation, but carnivorous nonetheless—lives endless as spirits, feasting upon flesh after flesh since war in heaven, generation following generation, even in mine—from father to daughter—a parasite, a problem, a pariah, a caustic curse

freemason curse

dad grew up
under freemason's curse
—the son who does not join
will be cursed
—a spoken promise
his mason father made
"the tongue has the power of life
and death"

word curse by brother's demonic dream
to brother
of a motor cycle death
body turned over
my dad

came true
three times
he should have died
rain

back story

under an overpass
hit by a car
flipped backward
helmet protected his head
preserving his life
left leg hanging
by skin's snippet
abundant bleeding, shock
two off-duty officers
tourniqueted his leg
preserving his life
ambulance nearby
hastily helped
preserving his life
with a snip
the leg was gone
a prosthesis slipped in place
pain never left
but God preserved him
dad
it was not his time
to die

> "The LORD, the LORD God, compassionate and gracious, slow to anger, and abounding in lovingkindness and truth; Who keeps lovingkindness for thousands, Who forgives iniquity, transgression and sin; yet He will by no means leave the guilty unpunished, visiting the iniquity of fathers on the children and on the grandchildren to the third and fourth generations."
> (Exodus 34:7)

the curse
unrepented
handed down
as a father's name
real
but intangible

unseen
what God reveals
repented
became broken
over me

"Christ redeemed us from the curse of the Law, having become a curse for us—for it is written, 'CURSED IS EVERYONE WHO HANGS ON A TREE.' " (Galatians 3:13)

the rhubarb

sweet cut rhubarb
sours my tongue
as i suck stem's simple sap
summer's growth tinted pinks
with leafy top's poison
chopped off
fresh taste of yesterday
curdling
until sugared and crisped
into melting memories
for quick looks back
when heart
aches with hurt

all things

"He will use it all"
flings my friend
the past
the good, the ugly, the hurt
the sweet, the sour, the poison

> "And we know that God causes all things to work together for good to those who love God, to those who are called according to His purpose." (Romans 8:28)

snow pile
(first published at *Everyday Poets*)

that winter was thick ice
forlorn shanties littered frozen tundra layered with
many days' snows

crinkled borders bounded by
blue-collar cottages
where a mill and log cabins
once squatted

the way to town, now empty
the rebuilt church—brick by
mortared brick

a stained glass image of Jesus
watching over

i scamper, slide, play
upon noon's pond

fire whistle blown
all left for home
fishermen, skaters,
not even a mother

wisdom without
hardly grown to be left alone
—a babe making snow angels

piled high nearby,   hidden from first sight
as all the lakeage appeared
color of innocence

back story

lopsided balls of snow
—as if a monument, such as Jacob's
reverence of holy ground—leading upward

this hallowed place beneath
great augured hole
gaping gulf for lines and lures
waiting to be observed, cleared
to swallow a child

finally noticed,
as if a pile of fallen leaves
from passed season
to a child's imagination
a delightful thought enters the mind: "run and jump!"

no caution, consideration
no call from a mother
i catapult forward
booted feet first
snow-suited body following
weight upon baby weight
gravity like quicksand,
water grasping tightly with its frigid arms

a violent stop
arms splayed wide as the angel's
one to the right
the other to the left
mittens scraping snow, friction melting ice
intervening grace, unseen

shock! beneath armpits, thick ice
all beneath the breastbone pulls
young life, sapping strength
breath by breath

Unbound

visible, as puffs of fog lifting from the white,
my hooded hatted head appears
to no one

danger innocently understood
life or death?
under   or   out?

storm windows latched against winds
piercing air
hearing only silence
numbness of body, of mind
"…must…get… out!"

i struggle, i push
strength given in time of need
crawling away,
soaked,   sopping,   sobbing
a life continues
at 4 years old

"Jesus asked the boy's father, 'How long has this been with him?' 'F*rom childhood*," he said. 'It often throws him into the fire *or into the water, trying to kill him.* But if You can do anything, have compassion on us and help us.'" (Mark 9:21-22)

"You *deaf and mute spirit*, I command you, come out of him and do not enter him again." (Mark 9:25)

spirits enter

children
to kill—
spirits speak to children
drawing them
to water
to fire
to dive and break a neck
to jump and drown
to fall
and not swim
to destroy

God preserved me
only by His power
did i live
only to His glory
shall i die

each night
knees bent
i pray the Word
protection
from satan's plots
against my children
my family
my mother
close friends
even enemies without the Lord
in a spiritual arena
pleading the Blood of Jesus
over them
a wall of Holy Spirit fire
a wall of Holy angels
placed around them

the power of
the Word

"He who dwells in the shelter of the Most High will abide in the
shadow of the Almighty. i will say to the Lord, 'My refuge and
my fortress, my God, in whom i trust.' No evil shall be allowed to
befall you, no plague come near your tent. For he will command
his angels concerning you to guard you in all your ways.
On their hands they will bear you up, lest you strike
your foot against a stone."
(Psalm 91:1,2,10-12)

the spot

at three
"she is so sensitive"

at four
under wood's steps
up and down
my spot
hidden
from parents' eyes

at six
under hanging little dresses
behind slatted doors
my spot
hidden
from mother's eyes

at ten
under sheets
tented overhead
my spot
hidden
from family's eyes

at twelve
behind closed doors
of solitude
leafed screens on boughs
behind puberty's face
lies shame
safely hidden
within my spot
false shame of who i am
false shame of what i was

"Therefore there is now no condemnation for those who are in Christ Jesus." (Romans 8:1)

false shame

as if a forward friend
enveloped me
kept close
until
i pushed it away
and cried
"no more!"
to the accuser of the brethren

back story

the talk

without boundaries
she grew
repeating what was heard
inside home's walls
until the talk
talked back
when neighbors gossip
and anger flares

without boundaries
her mother led
as she had learned
telling able listeners
her life
until the children
heard
about themselves
in talk
talk
that talked back
when parents gossip
and anger flares

the talk
which talks
and never ceases
rippling across ....gossips' party
line..
where children sit
to learn
and hurt
both when they
talk
and when they
listen

to the talk
the talk
that talks back

"The words of a gossip are like choice morsels; they go down to the inmost parts." (Proverbs 18:8)

boundaries

come from God
Who divided nations
peoples
languages
words
good
from evil
and He has taught me
separation from evil
even in words
edifying with good
fruit of the Spirit

"What is the outcome then, brethren? When you assemble, each one has a psalm, has a teaching, has a revelation, has a tongue, has an interpretation. let all things be done for edification."
(1 Corinthians 14:26)

interlude

reflection at 19

japan......1983
kneeling upon youthful knees
as if a japanese *geisha*
as all polite women under the rising sun do
on *tatami's* woven matting
i dare to see summer's long unseen reflection

like an adzuki sweet bean bun
body surrounded by cherry-blossom *yukata*
summer's sister flowered kimono
heron width-dropped arms
sashed waist, minus *obi*
clothing my youth
neck to ankle
in modesty

silently fingering simple earrings
on one-night loan from a co-patriot,
contraband conservatively prohibited
missionary holes just beginning to knit themselves
faster than the unnatural breaches in my girlish heart
i cast glances at the strange young woman
   reflected back

evening. silence. church goers bowed goodbyes home
ofuto bathing ending. meal finished.
retired to second floor's solitude
night of reflection
melancholic introspection
across the Pacific
across time
a meter's look into a mirror of life
at what 19 should be

interlude

eyes, void of makeup—speak of happiness
melancholia dissipated,
depression temporarily lifted
like bubbling beans in a pot
and life restored blossom cheeks
cooled and crushed with sweet sugar
wrapped within portuguese bread
pan
sweetness added
becomes the hidden treasure which only
the eater knows of

believer

baptism at sixteenth summer
believed He called me to go
missions became a moving sidewalk
a run away
avoiding home
fresh fruit fell full
God used me
where i ran

interlude

florida

followed graduation
a car, a highway, a plan
to run away
from hurt
finding love
finding first settlement
a husband, a home
God's help

"Be still, and know that I am God" (Psalm 46:10)

deeper

dad

was he saved?
i didn't know
but spent 35 years in prayer
to find the answer
days before he passed

i tried to find a cure, a therapy
no luck
his time of husbanding, dadding
at an end
pancreatic cancer at 65
it fell to me to administer his medication
attempting painlessness
until his spirit passed

prayer answered
in last days
"baptized in the baptist church"
he entered in
through pearled port
of heaven

my grief groaned and grew
"i'm sorry mom!
i couldn't save him!"
a three-year deepened depression
had begun
i carried within myself
the sentence of death

it is not

Holy Spirit led me
it is not the child's role
to take a sick parent to the Lord
but parent
who takes child
it was not my place to save my dad
but was his
to do for me

(Matt 15:21-28, 17:14-23; John 4:43-54)

how?

how did this happen?
i was a child who loved Jesus
a teen who accepted Christ
a missionary to japan
a Christian university graduate

how could this happen?
i was a mother
a tither
a Christian school teacher

i knew the Word
though not well enough
i knew the dangers
but became blinded to truth

like eve
i was deceived
wanting to believe what wasn't true

deeper

unlike unfallen eve
i was ill, weak, cursed, confused
and growing worse
pummeled from every side by a gauntlet
of attacks
i sought refuge in God
seeking Him in unholy ways
spiraling into mental collapse
under the hold
of the enemy
who pretended to be God

He says

I will never leave you
nor forsake you
He did not
God keeps His promises
He turns to help
the one who cries to Him

nicely nurse

hospice's nicely nurse
knocked at back door
a spiritual attack
as paper paraphernalia
appearing as a soothing song
about what happens when we die
death without God
death without sin, judgment, heaven, or hell

door opening

nicely nurse
only knocked
but i opened the door
opened the page
a daughter depressed, unsure, afraid
when i read the words
believed the words
i sinned

to the occult
death is as nothing
even a pleasure
all pass and continue on
a lie implanted when i was weak
a lie believed and was deceived
a lie, from the father of lies
first step inside deception's gate
to find where dad had gone

saul's search

saul went to search for the dead
inquiring of a psychic
God warns us not to do so
they are familiar spirits
a type of demon
we find instead
speaking what they know (1 Samuel 28:7)

death

for believers
is truly life
a passing possible
from here
to heaven
"whoever believes in me
though he die
yet shall he live"
there is no other life

occult

what is spoken is true
though difficult to the ears
for some

the occult plays on
flesh of the mind
flesh of the body (Romans 8:5-6)
demonic presence may be felt
seen, heard
even in signs
flickering lights
activity of satan
energy changes (2Thessalonians 2:9)
influence of satan (2Thessalonians 2:11)

the occult is a visible invasion
recognizable
psychic stores, botanicas:
as you drive by
bless them in the name of Jesus
and watch them close

strange incense to burn and cleanse
the house
sage
instead welcoming the enemy in

tarot cards do tell the fortune
like tea leaves, turkish coffee grounds
speaking of what will come
giving power to the enemy
to curse
words believed
words lived

horoscopes printed since
my youth
i recorded them
kept them
a new one written
telling of my death

voodoo, hoodoo, santeria
and many other names
the calling of the demons
out
spirits used for purposes
and power

akashic readers
believe that they commune
that is—hear from
guardians of the records beyond
earth's history of all events
like psychics
picking up words of
familiar spirits
demons in disguise

meditation
flung open a back door
that remained open
other spirits spoke

                                              "i want to possess you"

nothing hidden there
transcendental meditation
visualizing a golden orb
entering
minutes became hours
of emptying the mind
of thought
listening to a gong

deeper

kundalini—a coiled serpent resides at the base of the spine
a spirit of divination
a method of reaching spiritual enlightenment
guided visualization—beside a river
placing thoughts into a bag
throwing them away
and mindfulness—breathing-focused thought
meditation
begins with emptying the mind
opening the heart to anything other than God
may start with yoga
meditation
is not safe
opens "portals"
which are back doors
to demonic entrance

though coming as light
meditation is a pagan demonic practice
promoted by the medical establishment

i gave up this practice
to dwell upon the Word of God
whatever is true (Philippians 4:8)

self-hypnosis
leaves the mind under another's control
hypnosis
opens doors to the subconscious
demonic control

reiki
is not massage
but energy releases
demonic deception

hands hot
power felt
demons transferred

the occult is a blind invasion
missed in ignorance
heralded by "light workers"
who do "good"
like the white witch over the rainbow
like the psychic
who sees inside the minds of autistic children
calming them
teaching their parents
how to do the same

movement of human spirit
purposely
in the night, in meditation
to see inside another's life
to speak inside another's dream
and yes,
even to rape
power given by the demonic
to enter in where sin has made
an opening
witches riding broomsticks
before moon's glow
today called
astro projection
very real

the occult is witches, wizards, warlocks
high priests of satanic cults
mediums, spiritists, palm readers, fortune tellers
the occult is ordinary men and women
who have become involved
and don't know the way out

deeper

the occult is grown children hurt by abusers
looking for hope foolishly
the occult is a type of power to the powerless
the occult sits beside you in the church
is your neighbor, your friend, a pastor's wife
it was me

i ate as eve ate
from the tree of knowledge of good and evil
to eat what God has forbidden
is to die (Leviticus 20:27)
on earth
without repentance
the lake of fire
the second death
eve died spiritually that day
she began to die physically
except for the grace of Jesus Christ
i too would be dead

> "There shall not be found among you anyone
> who makes his son or his daughter pass through the fire,
> one who uses divination,
> one who practices witchcraft,
> or one who interprets omens, or a sorcerer,
> or one who casts a spell, or a medium, or a spiritist,
> or one who calls up the dead.
> For whoever does these things is detestable to the LORD;
> and because of these detestable things
> the LORD your God will drive them out before you.
> *"You shall be blameless before the LORD your God."*
> (Deuteronomy 18:10-13)

attacks

the attack
came not once
nor twice
but many ways
many times
as a voice
speaking in the night
as if God
as satan spoke to Lord Jesus (Matthew 4:7)
                              "vengeance is mine, sayeth the Lord"
also with hysterical evil laughter
cynically sneering
cursing me with names
        and heckling
               "she does not know she is the light of the world"

entering a dream
through sin's door
as God's angels do (Matthew 2:19)
to direct   "you have made a vow to God"
as an acquaintance
friended through the internet
comes with violent lust
spirits moving in the night
outside the body
not by God's will
but the work of
the enemy
which enters in
through a tunnel
of love?

filled with flowering flowers
of many hues
a tunnel
as if to heaven
time spent together
until head smashed to ground
face turned
the rape

doors

closed
latched
covered by the Blood
once open
portals
in sleep
attacks now only memories
even the rapes
"spiritual rape"
not true in flesh
only in the mind
felt in body
demons
seeking mental control
through fear and falseness

only Holy Spirit shall fill the human spirit (Acts 9:17)
only Holy Spirit should move my spirit (2Corinthians 12:2)
not even i may move my own (1Corinthians 3:23)

He gives sweet sleep
to His beloved (Proverbs 3:24)

death

why do i love you
why do i follow
your lure
as a fly to honey
lovely lyrics creeping
into the cochlear
"if i die young...."
romance
rooming in memory
an earworm
playing over and over
beauty
"lay me down on a bed of roses"
imagination created the scene
which began belief of
what would be
last will and testament
written
prepared
"send me away with the words
of a love song"[1]
of death—you drew me
with the taste of
sweet bitterness

---

[1] The Band Perry, "If I Die Young," 2010.

to live

and let myself
become
alive
when death had held me close

deeper

as a man embraces a woman
i had to push away
while egged on by enemies
saw myself
throat cut
upon the floor
the desire to destroy myself
lingered about my life

clinging to truth
i am deeply loved by God
and so are you

back doors

deceit

like eve
i bit the fruit
for knowledge
of good and evil—
though i thought all was good
because i wanted—
scratch that,
i needed to know
more—
more of what
eye has not seen
and so
demons
pretending to be
GOD
bid me bite
forbidden fruit
the draw
of darkness

there is a reason
why we cannot see
the spiritual world
with human eyes

some of it is evil
of this—i know
some of it is good
and He
is GOD

and when i awoke
from the spell
of the crafty serpent
i found myself

like eve
afraid
—even of God (Genesis 3:8)

outed by GOD
the enemy acted:
he turned
wrathful
a monster as
satan himself

a nightmare
i ran
to the only Truth
i knew
—JESUS

He healed this wound
and leads me gently
that i might
never fear Him again

back doors

there is a back door
it is the way of a thief
or a robber
who sneaks
into the house
to bind the owner
to take what is not his

his way comes
through guise
deceit
pretending another
as the wolf
was to red riding hood
so is the enemy
to the believer

the back door
opens easily
when it has been
taught
through yoga's
"open your heart"
and the "corpse"
new habits practiced
become auto-pilot

through meditation
breathing hypnotic
breath
and ears hear gonging,
chanting
reminders to
empty
      the mind

lending itself to
visualization
a golden bowl
like that of
transcendentalists
which pretends to take
problems away
to another place

these back doors
exist
where man cannot
see
but in the spirit

not one or two
but many, many
just as a tree of knowledge
of evil
has much fruit

opening—willingly
to the work
of demons
—to kill
—to steal
—to destroy
words
a little more personal
to kill my body
to steal my testimony
to destroy my family

these back doors
fly as flags
conflagrating first signs
smoke signals

accidentally begun
or even intentional
as arson at a church
but fires
none the less

in the night
dreams
of a serpent
biting my ankle
a warning
a warning
a warning
unheeded
for many years

    "My people perish for lack of knowledge" (Hosea 4:6)

sound mind

for God did not give us a spirit of fear
(that is from satan)
but of power
and love
and a sound mind (2Timothy 1:7)
think on His Word
both day
and night
know the traps
tricks
pitfalls
of the enemy

back door: meditation

entrance

i asked him in
and in meditation
opened a door
believing
he,
a spirit
of one like me
would do no harm
i thought to see
the world
through his eyes—
deceived
too late
he was inside
he said
to stay

                                          "i will never leave"

a lie

meditate

a word with more than one meaning
meditate—to think on something a bit
ruminate
chew it over and over
understand it
pray about it
memorize it
use it

a word with a hijacked meaning
meditate—to empty one's mind
to achieve oneness with the universe
to reach a higher level of consciousness
to find peace
all lies

> "Keep this Book of the Law always on your lips;
> meditate on it day and night,
> so that you may be careful to do
> everything written in it.
> Then you will be prosperous and successful." (Joshua 1:8 NIV)

back door: meditation

yoga

meaning "yoked"
neck and neck
hooked
connected
attached
united
joined
in spirit
from hinduism
thousands of gods
each stretch
a pose of worship
to a god
an idol
idol worship
idolatry
behind each idol
a demon (1Corinthians 10:20)
demon worship
yoga
yoked to demons
joined to demons
demonization

we are to be yoked
only to Lord Jesus
"take My yoke upon you
for I am meek" (Matthew 11:29)
be one with Him
in Spirit

heart

"open your heart"
instructor repeats
over
over
over
until even strong minds
comply
following instructions
as we as children
were taught

the heart
seat of emotions
a back door (John 10:1)
through which demons
enter
the soul
the mind

God does not give
a spirit of fear
but of power
love
and sound mind

love Him
with *all* your heart

back door: meditation

corpse

a pose
as if dead
splayed
upon the floor
a time
to empty
the mind
meditation
enemy access
for Christ came
to give us life
not death
for we are to have the mind
of Christ (1Corinthians 2:16)
renewed
with the washing
of the Word (Ephesians 5:26)

giving over

attention!
giving over
to music
chanting
breaths counted
repetition
of a mantra
giving up
self will
self-control
in body
in mind
in spirit
inducing a hypnotic state
the beginning of
yoked
the beginning of
bondage
it was for freedom
Christ set us free
do not be subject
again
to a yoke
of slavery (Galatians 5:1)

back door: meditation

meditation's roots

yoked to yoga
poses=worship
mantras—
a word repeated
to aid concentration
in meditation
rooted in hinduism
extended in buddhism
came to america
with walt whitman,
henry david thoreau
ralph waldo emerson
literary icons
influencing american youth
came to america
with immigration
spread across the country
in the digital age
satan is patient

> "Come out from them and be separate, says the LORD.
> Touch no unclean thing, and I will receive you."
> (2Corinthians 6:17 NIV)

kundalini

speaks of "awakening"
as if you've been asleep
as eve was
when she bit forbidden fruit
her eyes were opened
knowledge of evil
comes through kundalini

a sample:
kundalini yoga
meaning "coiled one"
is a serpent
a snake
a demon
this is the truth
but is hidden in the foreign tongue
used by yoga

dark knowledge
isn't cheap
most pay with shortened lives
mental scars
even physical scars
as i have;
deep occult practices
left behind
invite attacks
it is WAR
war until the death
of the believer
or until
demons are chained
in the abyss (Luke 8:31)

back door: meditation

"But you must not eat from
the tree of the knowledge of good and evil,
for when you eat from it you will certainly die." (Genesis 2:17)

transcendentalism

moving one's spirit
yoga's final destination
rising above the world
to heaven
as if a god
just as witches move
at night
the broomstick
you do not move your own
spirit
though occultists believe
they can
as do yogis
practitioners
this is false power
given by the
demonic
just as angels once
carried the faithful
to abraham's bosom (Luke 16:22)

only the Spirit of Jesus
should fill, seal, move
the human spirit
as He called paul up to Heaven
God moved him (2Corinthians 12:2)

back door: meditation

portals

in meditation
demons gain entrance
because of sin
idol worship in form
in mind
through portals occultists call them—
holes
openings
to take control
a little
a little more
until the full mind
is theirs
to kill
to steal
to destroy

entrances
such as cain's
sin crouching at the door
he knew
pushed against God
in rebellion
sin has desire (Genesis 4:7)
as does the demonic
as does the believer who knows
what is sin
and does it anyway (James 4:17)

entrances
for enemy access to life
to limb (Luke 13:10-13)
no matter what they're named
must be shut
through repentance (Acts 5:31)

and deliverance (Acts 16:16-18)
kept closed
by the Blood
and obedience
never opened again
noncompliance
creates unclean community (Matthew 12:43-45)
demons cast out
come again
to find an entrance in

ask God to show you your sin
repent
that satan will have no claim
to you
your life
your family

> "I will not speak much more with you,
> for the ruler of the world is coming,
> and he has nothing in Me." (John 14:30)

back door: meditation

chakras

meaning "wheel"
"circle"
a center of psychic energy
in the spirit
on the body—
where the two meet
openings
portals
for demonic entrance

disguised as
"self-discovery"
of what is dormant within
an "awakening"

giving false power
to "frog jump"
in the air
at various degrees
which is the moving of human spirit
referencing
telepathy
clairvoyance
psychic activity
remote viewing
"then i saw 3 impure spirits
like frogs
come out of the mouth
of the dragon" (Revelation 16:13)
false occult powers
helped by demons
supposed knowledge
of present, past, future
the work of familiar spirits
who steal

and lying spirits who lie,
only God knows the future,
to gain control over elements of the earth
weather
clouds
storms
as if by the power of self
even as the magicians in pharaoh's court
copied the works of God
i too am a witness to this
as are those in the occult
but greater is He Who is in me
than he who is in the world (1John 4:4)

back door: meditation

the 7

chakras count as 7
each has a mantra, a chant
each a residing god
each a new element of
demonic control over mind
until body obeys
sin: self above God
satan wins

the first called "muladhara"
meaning "root" or "support"
at base of spine
concentration first begins
hindus teach a serpent
lies coiled here
waiting to be awakened
ganesh, hindu god
here resides
ganesh
meaning "a group"
or "a categorical system"
and "lord and master"
kundalini yoga begins
with concentration
meditation
demons—
a group
organized in a system
enter
to reign
as lord and master
beginner's level

Jesus is Lord
you shall have no other gods
before Me—God (Exodus 20:3)

the second
svadhishthana
meaning "one's own base"
at the sexual organs
spirits of lust, whoredoms
play off the body, the mind
sins against self (1Corinthians 6:18)
brahma,
hindu god here resides
meaning "creator"
a lie
all things were made for Christ by Christ (Colossians 1:16)
the serpent—
the demonic team has risen higher
while the human believes
he's purifying his consciousness
raising his consciousness higher
the hub of subconsciousness
greater attacks occur at night, in dreams

the third chakra
called manipura
meaning "city of jewels"
lies at belly button's brush
here presides god
braddharudra
meaning
"power of destruction"
a demon
come to destroy (John 10:10)
a stolen life
the serpent

back door: meditation

gains more control
over body
over mind
more time in meditation
hours
the demon states

                                        "i will never leave you"

a lie
the true city of jewels
awaits the faithful
streets paved with gold
pearled gates
Christ enthroned
Heaven (Revelation 21:10-27)

the fourth
anahata
meaning "unbeaten"
and "pure"
belief in invincibility
placed at the heart
god
rudra shiva
here resides
he is "the roarer"
beware the enemy
who roars as a lion (1Peter 5:8)
telling you to
"follow your own heart
instead of Jesus"
—sergeant of satan
love the Lord
with all your heart (Luke 10:27)

chakra five
vishudda
meaning "especially pure"

at the throat
from here the demon speaks (Mark 5:9)
lies
threats
perverted truth
pan charaktra shiva
"god the destroyer"
resides nearby
in heart's center (Luke 22:3)
making it impure;
the serpent has wound itself
throughout the body
only head awaits
our bodies
are not our own
bought with a price
are the living temples
of the true God (1Corinthians 6:19)

the sixth
ajna
meaning
"perceive" or "command"
between eyebrows
called the third eye
proclaims it sees the future
hindi bindi
black dot adornment
impressions from the enemy
supposed knowledge
from both past, future
telepathy
only familiar spirits (2Chronicles 33:6)
who steal
and lying spirits (1Kings 22:23)
who lie
and spirits of divination (Acts 16:16)

back door: meditation

who pretend the future
divination's meaning
is "python"
a spirit that squeezes and crushes
to death

here is end of duality
male or female
light or dark
the end of separateness
the door is opened by ganesh
idol of the first chakra
who brings within
the organized system
of demonic parasites
residing god
ardhanarishvara
½ male, ½ female
transvestite
homosexual
his name means "lord"
he decides what the yogi practitioner will be
how he acts
how he thinks
perversion

> "Professing to be wise, they became fools,
> and exchanged the glory of the incorruptible
> for an image in the form of corruptible man
> and of birds and four-footed animals and crawling creatures.
> Therefore God gave them over in the lusts of their hearts
> impurity, so that their bodies would be dishonored among them.
> For they exchanged the truth of God for a lie,
> and worshiped and served the creature
> rather than the Creator, who is blessed forever. Amen.

> For this reason God gave them over to degrading passions;
> for their women exchanged the natural function
> for that which is unnatural,
> and in the same way also the men abandoned the natural function
> of the woman and burned in their desire toward one another,
> men with men committing indecent acts and receiving in their
> own persons
> the due penalty of their error.
> And just as they did not see fit to acknowledge God any longer,
> God gave them over to a depraved mind,
> to do those things which are not proper,
> being filled with all unrighteousness, wickedness, greed, evil"
> (Romans 1:22:-29a)

in the beginning God made
man and woman (Genesis 2:22)
and He called it good

the final chakra
seventh
sahasrara
meaning "thousand petaled"
as if a legion (Luke 8:30)
is topmost
crown chakra
upon the head
promising pure consciousness
but is only hell
promising self-realization finalized
but worship of man
his own consciousness
is sin, (Romans 1:22)
kundalini
the serpent
has risen to unite itself
with yogi
practitioner

back door: meditation

promising transformation to divine
and bliss
but is instead slavery (Romans 6:6)
kundalini wraps itself
around the head
as a crown
lord over its human host
to do whatever it wishes (Luke 8:27)
heavy
heavy
heavy
demonization
presiding deity
paramashiva
or "highest lord"
a demon who speaks

                                        "i will rule through you"

truly, truly
I say to you
he who does not enter
by the door
into the fold of the sheep
but climbs up
some other way,
he is a thief
and a robber (John 10:1)
satan is the thief
seeking to rob believers
of their lives in Christ

truth?

kundalini calls itself "truth"
"sacred"
and "the power of the love of God"
satan often comes as love
false love
to the rejected, the unloved
he comes as a pimp to a child
buying her candy
only to use her
this is yoga
the pimping of body and mind
of even believers
who without knowledge
of evil and death
submit themselves
doctors, hospitals, and science
preach the practice
healthy
beneficial
for lowering blood pressure
chronic pain,
these are the same
who have preached evolution
in schools
eroding Godly minds

yoga says
"ascending consciousness
leads to divine"
man cannot ascend to God
Babel is not forgotten (Genesis 11:1-8)

back door: meditation

God comes down to men
as the Bread of Life
the Word of God
as Lord Jesus
because of His great love
and mercy

yoga calls itself
"the narrow path"
a fakery
millions are meandering
the broad boulevard
downward to darker darkness (Luke 11:34-35)

yoga believes
that people are
the eternal spirit
not God Himself (Genesis 1:1; John 1:1)
sin

7 chakras
7 is the Biblical number of completion
even this
back doors to enemy control
is a lie
every sin opens a door to enemy capture
of human territory

becoming psychic centers
which affect the mind
emotions
the will
subconscious: night dreams
and false visions by day
appearing as lunacy, insanity, craziness

Lord Jesus
Son of God
Who came of a virgin once
Who died on the cross
rose from the grave
and ascended to Heaven
is the true Door (John 10:9)
open only to Him
He knows your name
and leads you
as a shepherd leads
his sheep
to abundant life

back door: meditation

symbols

the om
powerful chant
three sounds
for three gods
brahma, shiva, vishnu
unholy trinity
a copy of true Trinity
behind each god a demon
known as a goddess, an energy
brahma
creator of universe, hindu texts
shiva
destroyer and recreator of the universe
vishnu
preserver, protector

the chant
the om
the calling to demons
to come
back doors open
with the om
for 3 to enter in

the lotus
a different daisy
for each chakra
as kundalini
the serpent
rises
with meditation
upon body's location
the demon opens

blossom's bloom
kissed with a hiss
another portal
for demonic entry

hamsa
the hand
pointing 2-thumbed down
false protection
evil eye's center
welcomes enemies inward

mandala
circles within circles
of unending universe
absorbs the mind
in meditation
consumed
tasty tidbits for the darkness

buddha
meaning "awakened one"
idol
a man who too
was deceived
and used
to deceive millions more
lies dead

symbols
pictures
tattoos
have meaning
look only to the cross
and Him crucified (1Corinthians 1:22-23)

back door: meditation

kalki

vishnu,
false god of unholy trinity
believed
will return to earth in troubled times
to restore balance between good
and evil
incarnated nine times
a tenth
at world's close
false Christ (Matthew 24:23-25)

hindus
call him "kalki"
he will arrive
and usher in an age of truth

kalki
meaning "white horse, eternity, destroyer"
will sit upon a horse of white
with fiery sword
false Christ (Matthew 24:4-5)
Lord Jesus will not be reincarnated
the Lord will come from heaven
with fire in His eyes (Revelation 19:11-13)
as He left
in a physical glorified body
with nail prints on hands, feet
hole in His side (John 20:24-29)
to the mount of olives (Zechariah 14:4)
in the presence of His disciples (Revelation 19:14)
with the sound of the trumpet! (1Corinthians 15:52)
God from heaven!

believer
do not look toward evil
flee from it
why do you seek
the Living One among the dead?

kalki is an *avatar*
modern word?
no
old and borrowed
avatar—
one who has power
to take on any form
at will
a reincarnation
of spirit in flesh
only God has the power
of incarnation
it was once
2,000 years ago
Baby Jesus
born in Bethlehem
no human
no creation
may take on any form
as an avatar
at will

reincarnation

the belief that life
cycles
the soul
again and again
until made ready
purified
to ascend
as a god
into heaven

> "Therefore, having these promises, beloved, let us cleanse
> ourselves from all defilement of flesh and spirit, perfecting
> holiness in the fear of God." (2Corinthians 7:1)

past lives lived
a belief held by
all religions worldwide
outside God's church
is pagan and ancient
is false

the occult teaches
that we choose our
weaknesses, illnesses, diseases
before we're born
overcoming them
raises the human soul
to a higher spiritual plane
in the next life

> "For all have sinned and fall short of the glory of God."
> (Romans 3:23)

eastern religions call it karma
what one did in past lives
decides his fate in this life
and future lives

a belief that is cheap
eugenics becoming common sense
abortion made easy
there will be many more chances

a belief that
each person has three outs
when life becomes unbearable
three opportunities
to choose death
even suicide

satan's lie of
reincarnation
exists
to devalue human life
to deceive many
about the return of Christ
allowing for many
to come in His name
and lead astray
even the elect (Luke 21:8)
into apostasy
there is only one life
and then
the judgment (Hebrews 9:27)

deep things

deep things

of satan
unknown to those
grown up inside church walls
who have not walked the walk
daily downward
one step
       another
              three steps
                        into utter darkness

my intimate time with satan
took me behind closed gates
to see
what he was doing
and join in his work

i thought him to be a loving
benevolent father
as if God
but could not love
just own
giving me what my flesh desired
promising lies
even his voice cannot be misunderstood
it is a false love
as a man tells a child
"i love you"
only to molest her

the image is not easy to imagine
my apologies
but the deep things are ugly
leading to mind control
bodily control
and finally death

deep things

we are to know the plots of satan
and not be deceived (2Corinthians 2:11)
expecting God to expose them (Ephesians 5:11)
He saves us
to the uttermost
even from behind enemy lines

the occult

what is secret
what is hidden
what lifts its head up
above God

practices
supernatural
paranormal
mystical
pagan
magical

copies of God's work
magicians of egypt
did the same
a river of blood
with their secret arts (Exodus 8:7)

replicas
false
made to look like truth
even satan may come
as light (2Corinthians 11:13-14)

God's wonders
satan's false wonders
apparitions
ghosts
orbs
voices
visitations of the dead
or angels
through demons

movement of human spirit
in a dream or vision
as real as this book
as real as this paper

prayer to a demon
bowing on knees
before a false vision of Christ
coming through an open door
down steps

laying on of hands
      passing of a demon into the body through prayerful hands
speaking in tongues
      demonic language
prophet and prophecy
      false prophet, false prophecy
laying of hands for healing
      false healing, unlasting

i have learned caution
words have meaning
hands intent
caution
caution
caution

satan comes as God the Father
he comes as God the Son
he comes as Holy Spirit
he comes as if he himself is God Almighty

the Door of Jesus
    back doors, false Jesus:
        jehovah's witnesses: Jesus is not son of God, only an angel
        hindus: await a false Christ
        santeria: do not follow Christ, but a demon behind a false
            Christ
        islam: Jesus is not son of God, but a prophet, who will
            return
so many back doors
endless
know Jesus, the True Door
"I am the Way, the Truth, the Light"
there is only one way to God
His Way: Lord Jesus (John 14:6)

inside the church

false teachers enter in
to Bible studies
churches
to interrupt
to take control
when they hear

                                        "speak! speak!"

an enemy speaks
to pervert and twist the truth
and i have seen
believers
of many years
accept that Christ will come
again
as He did at first
an infant
—a lie believed
because of the argument:
Jews themselves were looking for the Messiah
not an infant in Bethlehem
will we misunderstand Scripture
again?

that false teacher was praised
raised
welcomed
practically commissioned

many false teachers will go out
in His name (2Peter 2:1)
do not follow them
know the Word of God
and believe it

heavily demonized come to speak
as prophets, leaders
discernment is required
pray for this
pray the Lord expose the wicked (Ephesians 5:11)

a false prophet came to a church
he gave information
as a psychic gives
unedifying
he heard from familiar spirits
in him
the spirit of divination
a demon
and others
he laid hands and prayed
a friend, weak in elder age
deceived
felt falseness's touch and prayer
attacked
fell hospital ill
later died

another fought her way in
with false marriage
application to membership
developing division
cursed an elder's child
but she was exposed

these people
their eyes (Matthew 6:22)
a window to what is at work
within

deep things

the mind
looked out
malevolently
and spoke
words not their own

others
demonized but unknowing
because of meditation
and open doors
and ignorance
wrote of God's great works
to publish in church's book
falseness
lent by satan

and seek to open classes
on the equality of islam
the exercise of yoga
across the culture of the church
the Word of God
is not fully believed
every Word
every Scripture
did moses really fast 40 days? (Exodus 34:28)
can any man? (Matthew 4:2)
yes
i know those who do
and with great strength,
the blinding of satan
through western culture
cuts and slices off belief
one piece
at a time

endless list
church's boundaries have come down
because of ignorance
and ground's been given
to the adversary
to keep many from the Lord's love

spirits

satan and his demons
are spirits
without physical bodies
they neither give nor are given
in marriage
they do not procreate (Matthew 22:30)

they cannot produce
a race of giants
only men are created
by men
after his own kind
this is a law of God (Genesis 1:12, 21, 24-25)
Who makes us
He will not allow
physical sex with satan

demons will use others
for sexual attacks—rape
a sin
sad to say
the receiver, the victim
may receive a demon (Romans 1:27)
in the act
even a child

for fornication
sex outside marriage
of any type (Leviticus 18:22, 20:13; 1Corinthians 6:9)
a door is opened
to the demon of lust
whoredoms

as a man thinks in his heart
so he is
where are immoral thoughts from?
lust of the flesh
the enemy plays upon this
tempting

                                              "do i want this?"
                                              "do i like this?"
                                              "take him"

but the marriage bed
is undefiled
no enemy may be transferred
during the joining of a husband and wife (Hebrews 13:4)

deep things

roulette

dad lay dying
without death's desire

knees bowed upon tile
head tilted forward
hands tightly clasped
i desperately prayed
"oh Lord, i feel like
dad's life is in my hands
he is dying
but he wants to live
show me Lord,
how shall i prepare him
to live or to die?"

closing eyes
opening the book
i stuck in my finger
striking the word
"death"
Psalm 23
yea, though I walk
through the valley of the shadow
of <u>death</u>

in a weak moment
the beginning of magic
of wanting to know more

the Bible became my ouija board
improper usage
biblical magic
without study
led to God's enemies—
influence

upon God's child
in my weakest
time of need
who pandered themselves
as God
Himself
demonic guidance came
by a finger
a word
twisted
by the spirit of divination

anything can be used for magic

the book

these words
from the enemy
i recorded
with demonic dreams
and false visions
in a notebook
becoming precious

books of dark arts
knowledge of darkness (Acts 19:19)
open doors to demon's activity

in childhood
1970s comic books advertised occult things
fairytales of witches from library's shelf
1990s potter books
satan seeks hellish sentences early
making magic normal
now there are zombie fish books
for preschool
this is akin to voodoo

like a serpent about the neck
satan seeks to control
how a child thinks
what he likes
what he does (Mark 9:24-26)

occult books
are in libraries
book shops
even church thrift stores
accessible to ereaders
to open is the beginning of a downward descent
a draw to darkness

until Bible is set aside
church attendance left behind
worship music hurts the ears

> "But if you do not drive out the inhabitants of the land,
> those you allow to remain will become *barbs in your eyes*
> and thorns in your sides.
> They *will give you trouble*
> in the land where you will live." (Numbers 33:55)

a house
must be cleaned of books and movies
about fairies
gnomes
werewolves
the paranormal
supernatural
ghosts
false religions
witchcraft
any word that opposes the knowledge of God (2Corinthians 10:5)

not to be given away
but burned—
in Ephesus
many of those
who practiced magic
brought their books
together
and began burning them
in the sight of everyone
and they counted up the price of them
and found it
50,000 pieces of silver
several million dollars (Acts 19:19)

deep things

no matter the cost
your life
your children's lives
are worth more
than books,
while they remain
within the home
there is an opening
for demonic activity
a draw to darkness
near crib's cry

the stone

"keep this
it will protect you"
the psychic handed a stone
i took it
a charm, a fetish, a talisman
blessed by evil
feeling funny
tossed to trash

cursed are these and any item
keeping company with the occult
tarot cards
sage to smudge (Jeremiah 19:4 NIV)
totems
idols
special candles
incense (Jeremiah 1:16 NIV)
religious statues
mythological pictures
even
a simple stone

like a voodoo doll
with pins
an item meant
to bring a curse upon the keeper
demons
come through a curse (Romans 6:16)

God says,
you shall have no other gods before Me (Exodus 20:3)
the fetish for protection becomes a god
it is sin
the only true protection is God
His banner over me is love

my friend

i held my arms out
fingertips stretched
she rang the bells
from crown to toes
invoking deities
invoking Jesus
yes, even Jesus
to cleanse me from evil
to protect me from enemies
evil spirits
before i left her house

my good friend
who worked with "good spirits"
blind to their badness
cursed—
murderer chased
roofie victim
husband drugged her
daughter
caught in a gang,
tarot reader—
she called cards
demons
to speak of future events
familiar spirits (1Samuel 28:7 KJV)

my good friend
grandmother
loving woman
deceived
her daughter working
in a doctor's office
traveled to cassadega
psychic capital of the world

witches' den
at mother's request
a psychic prophesied
                "you will be involved in nerve disease research"
counted a blessing
new work her mother claimed
two months later
diagnosed
cursed
became a patient for
nerve disease research
daughter of
my good friend

as deep calls to deep (Psalm 42:7)
so too the darkness in me
drew me to others
who also held darkness dear

do not turn to mediums
psychics
do not seek them out
and so make yourself
unclean by them
I am the Lord your God (Leviticus 19:31, 20:6 KJV)

the occult
is not for fun
it is certain death (1Chronicles 10:13 KJV)
and lifts itself as a hypnotizing black serpent
holding your children in its gaze
because of choices
parent makes (2Chronicles 33:6 KJV)

the heart

center of emotions,
thoughts, feelings,
desires, appetites, passions
whether good or evil
the mind
where spiritual life begins
with choice

spirits watch, listen
for weakness
opportunity
to tempt (Daniel 10:12-13; Matthew 4:3)

with words
as if a thought, (Matthew 16:21-23)
without discernment (1Corinthians 12:10)
captured to Christ (2Corinthians 10:5)
temptation
is considered
chewed on
as if bubble gum

the power of death
is in the tongue (Proverbs 18:21)
words taken
spoken
used
allow satan
to enter in
to fill the heart
smother the mind

as happened to ananias
satan filled his heart
to lie to Holy Spirit
the price
death (Acts 5:3-5)

as happened to his wife
complicit
she too lied
the price
death (Acts 5:7-10)

sin is contagious
affecting those close to us
who out of love
participate
who out of greed,
lust for public praise
lying, hypocrisy, and pride
in effective rebellion
against God

satan is at work among believers
tempting
to enter the heart, the mind
where weakness reigns
to choose to follow him
instead of God
the price
death

the heart should be filled
with knowledge of God
as stephen's was (Acts 6:5,8)
as Lord Jesus' is
His Word, His Spirit
God Himself (John 10:30)

abyss

demons' darkness depths
sealed
locked
all go in
at Jesus' command
demon dread (Luke 8:31)

none come out
prison
under earth
in spirit
a shaft to surface
emits smoke when opened (Revelation 9:1-2)
as if a geyser
blowing steam
and water
from earth's bowels

abyss
with the king
over other evil spirits
apollyon or abaddon (Revelation 9:11)
which means "destruction"
all kept by God
until lucifer
is given a key
to open
end of age

readings

a word from the afterlife
loved one
gone beyond

a word about the future
what is coming
happy/sad

through mediums, clairvoyants,
fortune tellers, akashics
palm readers, i ching
astrology horoscope writers
spirit guides
tea leaves and coffee ground readers
through ouija board
tarot cards, runes
animal intestines
all are forms of divination
all are sin
all bring a curse

within my town
near old indian ground
boomed a business
a psychic circle
where meetups meet
for food and fellowship
weak people
empty lives and spirits
like my own
looking for more
or an experience

deep things

psychic led
she acknowledged her good spirit by name
whose energy moved the lights
a mother
she spoke of her children
how they too are psychically gifted
gauged, used
she spoke of churches
who denounce her work
they do not know the truth

a guinea pig came out of hat
he sat
we each closed eyes
to see what we could "see"
many saw wonderful things
to "bless" him with
but i saw a black cloud
and said so
and i was not welcomed back

> "So *Saul died* for his trespass
> which he committed against the LORD,
> because of the word of the LORD which he did not keep;
> and also because he asked *counsel of a medium*,
> making inquiry of it." (1 Chronicles 10:13)

a spiritualist camp
complete with "church"
inhabits woods outside
orlando
called
"psychic capital of the world"
believe in speaking

to the dead
but not to Jesus
cassadega
begun in western new york

my great great great grandfather
his obituary read
he was a spiritualist
able to see and speak
with his own dead
he too
born in western new york

drawn to divination
from family weakness
generations of iniquity
piled upon each other
as great heaped up garbage
my friend took me
claiming "good spirits"
"fun"
afraid—i toughed it out
and traveled twice

the spirit-filled hotel
hollered hollow
empty
yet eeriness lurked in shadows
speaking silently
hidden
a witch on a broom
pointed the way up stairs
a bad omen
she said
"evil spirits"

deep things

i threw good money
into two readings
the first
from a glassy-eyed gal
on hotel's top floor
mirrors on the window
facing outward
to keep away evil
the irony

here midnight séances
ensconce
voices from beyond
tourists shoot orbs with candid cameras

psychic prayer began each session
a head bow to her demons
she saw me waving a white flag
of defeat, surrender
she saw a girl come into the room
twice she stated
emphatically
that i was going to the white house
and called me a "savior"

do you see it?
the setting me up for
defeat
the giving up to control
the glamorous glib of going
to be important, famous
do you see it?

familiar spirits follow families
generations
knowing what humans cannot know
stealthily stealing

giving to the medium
to convey
as if a dead relative
dad, my child, my grandparent
sister, brother
were speaking

many grieve wrongly
looking for one lost
especially lost children
who are not truly lost
only gone to heaven
to be with the Lord
Jesus said,
"let the children come to me
the kingdom of heaven is theirs" (Matthew 19:14)

another medium
identified by name
his demon of divination
as if a woman
long dead in poland
he spoke little
prayed a spirit of divination in
with the laying on of hands
and urged me to leave Jesus
off my writing

not long afterward
i returned home
i dreamed a dream
in bed
the female psychic entered in
to sit beside
and remind me of the past
age 17

                        "God has made a promise to you and…"

deep things

i finished her phrase
answering without thought
pushed
egged
as if another spoke through me
"and i have made a promise to God"
a familiar spirit
who knew my pledge to go
to follow God
"i have decided to follow Jesus,
no turning back, no turning back"

beside me lay a woman
a name above her head
"dame saunders"
founder of hospice
dame of death

the door of my mind
opened to the psychic
and her demons
when i entered her room
bowed my head
she came later
as a witch upon a broomstick
in the night
astro-projection
as demon led
even forced her to do
why?
to lead a sheep further astray
toward death

beware the prayer
with anyone
or alone
to anything, anyone

other than God
in the Name of His Son
Lord Jesus

do not be led to prayer
with other faiths
entering their services
rituals

beware the prayer
outside the boundary
which brings the curse
upon the body and the mind
more blindness

> "You cannot drink the cup of the Lord and the cup of demons; you cannot partake of the table of the Lord and the table of demons." (1Corinthians 10:21)

i gave my first reading
pretended fortune-telling
gypsy-covered
halloween
age 12

in the middle east
coffee grounds
left to dry upside down
demitasse cups
were read
divination
towards me
a barely one-year bride

deep things

my mother met a fortune-teller
grandma and great grandma
saw psychics
though i never knew

after the divination door opens
the mind is compelled
more easily
the will given
toward abortion (Deuteronomy 18:10)
suicide
curses sticking

one more
akashic
a reader of the world's records
every soul
every thought
from every incarnation
kept in the spiritual realm
satan's false copy of the book of life
and God's books (Daniel 7:10; Revelation 20:12)

akashic means "heaven"
hindu,
idea extended by buddhism
here false tales
of the childhood of Jesus
originate

a beautiful smile
kindness
this reader
comes as light
in league with lucifer —disguised (2Corinthians 13-15)
she attends unity "church"
another form of strange spiritualism

i come prepared
a list of questions
she closes eyes
and hears from
"guardians of the records"
repeating what i'd heard in cassadega
a familiar spirit
no guardian
called me a reincarnation of a nun
who burned to death
at nazi hands
lying spirit spoke
and she spoke
       "in heaven, you are loved beyond your imagination"
difficult to depart from that
true of God
but perverted by spirits (Isaiah 19:14)
for their own gain
as if the guardians loved me
there are no guardians
no ancestors who speak
no catalog of records

akashic readings
used to help one understand
life's purpose

experts speak of psychics, mediums
and the like as frauds
charlatans
but every one i met was real
receiving communications
from the demonic

to call them fake
is to weaken them
cause to seem of no effect

deep things

danger
for those
like me
who wanted to "experience"
the paranormal

boundaries against psychics (Deuteronomy 18:10-12a)
are from God
given for our protection
we are here for His purpose
to glorify Him
and His Son (Isaiah 43:7)

cassadega

cassadega began as a spiritualist camp
southern extension
of the spiritualist "church"
from cassadega, new york

cassadega
a seneca indian name
a spirit guide
a demon
masked as the dead
cassadega manifested
made itself known
at a séance
exposing itself to medium john colby
instructing him to go to florida
take territory

along cassadega lakes in western new york
sit several indian mounds
formed by ancient ancestors
of today's tribes
holding skeletons
ritual fire beds
a long lost city
surrounding likely temple mound

iroquois, seneca forced out
1848 europeans moved in

since 1879 spiritualists hold the territory
pilgrimage plot
called lily dale

deep things

aboriginal occupations
original intents
for worship of deities (1Kings 11:5)
for divination
with human sacrifice (Leviticus 18:21)
litter the united states
spiritual territories held (Daniel 10:13)
after sin set in (2Kings 23:13)
allowed by God

just as jericho's foundation
rebuilt
son within
a sacrifice
its gates
the cost of the youngest son
their father
ahab (1Kings 16:34)
cursed places (Joshua 6:26)

from these locations
spirits influence territory
surrounding mounds
to kill, steal, destroy
you will see satanic signs in the physical
reflection of the spiritual
spiritualism,
witchcraft
masonic activity
past slavery
pedophilia
and fetishes for evil

legion bowed before Lord Jesus
demons begged not to be driven out
out of their territory
tombs by the lake
they entered new hosts
swine (Mark 5:1-20)

to enter in to spiritual conflict
upon an indian mound
is dangerous
yes, paul preached from mars hill (Acts 17:22)
but paul was a chosen vessel of God
to carry the Gospel to gentiles
he suffered for it

spiritual conflict on a mound includes
completing a building
praying
preaching
singing
attempting to cast out demons
and even walking the mound
it is enemy territory

to enter warfare
without God's direction (Judges 4:4-7)
permission
essentially is sin
is to invite enemy attack (Revelation 12:17)
a curse
—like a mosquito truck spraying
pesticide
over your baby
over your food

miscarriage
autism
drug addiction
death
upon the children
first born

as God struck down firstborn of egypt
against the gods of egypt (Psalm 135:8)
so too does satan
from within his territory
where there is cause

it is warfare
in the spiritual realm
affecting or acting through
the physical realm
it is very very real

for unrealized sin
repent
ask for God's mercy
forgiveness
break the curse
ask for God's protection
from death's demonic angels

aliens

from beyond beings began
our beginnings
fables formed
for extraterrestrials
aliens
in unidentified flying objects
saucers
as superman arrived
as martians came
as many movies' magic manifests
across screens
images
embedded upon memory

the demonic dallies with devices
of fear, control
as a cat plays with its mouse
before killing it
night invasions by body snatchers
temporary paralyzation
taken away in spaceships
all impressions by demons
mind control
on those unclean
open to demonism
at night
an invasion of the subconscious
using familiar memories, images, thoughts

aliens do not exist
though many believers believe, wonder, consider
even churches choose to
an unholy hoax

a great ungodly worldwide deception
by satan
god of this world (2Corinthians 4:4)
power of the air (Ephesians 2:2)

adam and eve (1Corinthians 11:7, 15:47 NLT)
created by God (Genesis 1:27)
the last of His creation
in *His* image
the crown—the plan
to wear the crown (2Timothy 4:8)
as sons of God (Galatians 3:26)

man
made to rule over all the earth
it was very good (Genesis 1:28-31)
everything in the universe
completed
stars, planets
everything
God stopped (Genesis 2:1-2)

"For the time will come when people will not put up with sound doctrine. Instead, to suit their own desires, they will gather around them a great number of teachers to say what their itching ears want to hear. They will turn their ears away from the truth and turn aside to myths." (2Timothy 4:3-4 NIV)

healing

the prescription

like a bottle
top popped
spilling pills
across kitchen's counter
others
fall to floor
to roll and lie
with dust, dog hair, dirt

medicine
medical care
therapies
both good and evil
come out of the same office
the doctor who prescribes
both medicine and yoga
the hospital which authorizes
both surgery and meditation
the psychiatrist who
practices past-life regression
paired with hypnosis on his patients
then recommends
less stressful work
the physical therapist who utilizes
weight-bearing exercises
and acupuncture

hospitals and hospice
now specialize in spiritual care
for anyone
to anything
by many who do not know the Lord
rightly refuse those
you do not know
some only pretend to know the Lord

boundaries must be kept
against forms of the occult
physical attacks
in the name of medicine
healing
unclean spirits
demons
which enter in

acupuncture
needling the body
for reduction of pain
from pagan religion tao
meaning
"the way, path, route, road"
many gods
for seeking enlightenment
spiritual perfection
the practice of divination
"i ching"
beliefs in yin and yang
negative and positive forces
in the world, in the body

acupuncture
seeks to bring yin and yang
into harmony
with movement of the qi
"one's life force"
an energy
that flows along pathways
called meridians
connecting acupuncture points
even reaching
internal organs

healing

each acupuncture point
has specific diseases
associated with it
each acupuncture point
is an access
for unclean spirits—energy
a bowing to the tao

qi is satan's copy
the true life force is not a demon
but the Lord Jesus
in Him all things
hold together (Colossians 1:17)
He says,
"I am the Way, the Truth and the Life"

edgar cayce

a medium who spoke of akashic records
from where he received knowledge
both past and future
was called "the sleeping prophet"

as a child he played with the "little people"
and had an angel visitation

cayce entered trances at will
demons gave him information
to "help" the ill
his secretary took notes
publishing many books
don't open them
dangerous is that desire

cayce was the founder of the new age era

edgar read the Bible every year
and was a sunday school teacher
his parents had taken him to church
he thought to help others
especially sick children
as a missionary

cayce's evil work began
with hypnotism
for healing
of his own

the back door opened
led him away from God
an instrument of satan
his work still destroying others

healing

satan comes to pervert God's will
using demonic knowledge deceptively to heal
taking entire families away (2Peter 2:6)
to hell

deceived he spoke of polygenism
man began with five human races
various colors
spread across the earth
simultaneously

deceived he spoke of aliens, atlantis
and gave incorrect predictions

cayce was satan's copy of a disciple in a trance
as peter was (Acts 10:10, 11:5)
praying in the Spirit (Jude 1:20)

which spirit do you pray in?
to whom?
to God, His Son Jesus, in Holy Spirit
or falsely,
in the realm of spirits

God is our healer
He leads us not into temptation
not into hypnotism
which opens demonic doors
not even for healing

desperate
parents took their daughter
unable to walk
to a doctor
he kept her two weeks
chanting over her
sacrificing animals

forced her to drink their blood
traumatizing
a taste of voodoo
a witch doctor

santeria
voodoo's saintly sister
seeks the same
prayer to a saint
for cancer's cure
prayer by paid priest
who sacrifices blood
who bows not to God
nor even saints
but prays to demons
within himself

when my son was a child
a doctor told me he would not live
desperate
i tried acupuncture
diet
herbs
in the end
bowed knees
nightly
beside his bed
God has raised him
and kept satan's curse
from off his head

a child beside me
cursed with cancer
recurring
remembered in past prayers
faithful father
mother

healing

calling to God
a prayer was prayed
in the Spirit
and with understanding
to break curse's hold
she lives

enemy *attacks*
both mind and body
to make lame
paralyzed
cause convulsions (Mark 1:26)
mental illness
cancer
disease
where there is weakness
satan moves
against generational curse
generational iniquity
genetic problem passed in DNA
against present illness
made worse

he hates
and will not show deference
not even to children

deaths
disease
unnecessary
My people perish
for lack of knowledge (Hosea 4:6)

great is God,
the duty of parents
as the woman who brought her daughter (Matthew 15:22-28)
to Jesus
as the man who brought his son (John 4:47)
to Jesus
great is God

infusion

as blood plasma
transfused
by doctors

so does God transfuse
His Holy Spirit
as given to samson (Judges 14:6)
against enemies
as given to Lord Jesus (Luke 3:22)
for 40 days fasting
power against satan (Mark 1:13)

a false infusion
of power
as energy
heat
like tingling electricity
a feeling
fulfilling lust of flesh
weakness
coming from enemy entrance

"i will infuse you"

arriving through touch
watchword: <u>energy</u>
arriving without touch
through demonic activity already in play
believers beware

only God truly dispenses
Godly power
Godly healing
belongs to the Lord

energy

of healers applying energy
beware
refuse
rebuke
therapeutic touch
cranial work
acupuncture
acupressure
healing touch
reiki
shamanism
qi gong bodywork
chi kung
aura healing
chakra healing

the energy is real
tangible
felt
hot
coming through the laying on of hands
satan's copy of God's true healing (James 5:14-15)

i sat upon her couch
her hot hands pressing
against my thigh's flesh
stereo flickered on and off
she worked with spirits
upon my legs
a reiki practitioner
afterward
tingling
with weakness
as if i'd drunk a beer

healing

where does the energy come from?

practitioners practice
daily
using visualization
calling in the energy
just as voodoo and santeria priests beat drums
to call in spirits
demons come
their presence is as energy
heat
demons come from the earth (Job 1:7)
and from the air (Ephesians 2:2)
as they are called into the body

demons flow through healers
transference
a channel to receivers
a copy of Holy Spirit
working through a believer (2Timothy 2:21)

santeria priests are admitted in a miami hospital
reiki in more than 60 hospitals
reiki education available in 800 plus
30,000 nurses in U.S. hospitals use "touch"
energy practices each year
satan's copy
God's people—
nurses who serve the Lord

unity

a "church"
like tea
steeped in mysticism
with mindfulness and meditation
for searching souls without rest
in need of quietness

former believers
many found acceptance
employing "functional Christianity"
Jesus no longer Lord
relegated to bookstore shelves
catalogued with other great prophets

every seat taken
chuckling children chuck the aisle
forward
leader's hands upon them
in blessing
satan's copy of the Lord
not forsaking little ones (Mark 10:16)

discipleship, sanctification
the how
the why of letting go
the need of enlightenment
even the children are taught
to meditate

the church all sang rounds
emptying minds
in search of healing
finding none

healing

stay close to Lord Jesus
abide in Him
and He will abide in You
there is no true spiritual healing
no peace
apart from Lord Jesus

> "And he will be called Wonderful Counselor,
> Mighty God, Everlasting Father,
> Prince of Peace."
> (Isaiah 9:6b)

out!

unclean spirits
ordered out
each cried out
with reluctance
obeyed
with convulsions
obeyed

lame walked
paralyzed moved
blind saw
deaf heard

great is the power of Holy Spirit
as He flows through
the Word
He is in the voice of the believer
by the Name of Jesus
demons depart
healing is made

only Lord Jesus heals body, mind, spirit (Matthew 12:15)
only Lord Jesus can cleanse unclean spirits
causing sickness
causing death

"In Him was LIFE, and the life was the Light of men." (John 1:4)

war

a military

pastors preach
we are born into a war
between good and evil
God and satan
Light and darkness

yet when a believer dies
we ask God
"why?"

satan secrets his methods
through spiritual blindness
layered on
as if a slow growing
continuous cataract
over generations

war means military organization
from top to toes upon earth's dirt
satan, lucifer
fell from heaven because of sin (Luke 10:18 NIV)
many angels left with him

he is ruler over all his kingdom
he is prince of power of the air (Ephesians 2:2)
not everywhere
but he is one single spirit being
who has eyes and ears
like the CIA, FBI, NSA
in many places

to not believe
that he is real
is blindness (2Corinthians 4:4)
this too is satan's will

war

our struggle (Ephesians 6:12)
is not against
flesh and blood
but against rulers
which means "arche"
greek for *highest angels*
those with satan
in ranks

against powers
which means "exousia"
greek for *authorities*
with delegated influence
jurisdiction
these are the forces of the air
in satan's spiritual realm

against world forces of darkness
which means "kosmokrator"
down on earth
in orderly arrangement
as an army
with great strength to lay hold
and to keep
these are territorial spirits
though on earth
a part of the kingdom of darkness
hidden in shadows
whose purpose it is to keep or bring
areas
communities, cities
into greater darkness—blindness
—removal through temptation and sin
of church leadership
—closing of churches

they are as a cohort, battalion, band
of the roman army
garrisoned to protect provinces
as rome's empire was
in significant locations
for example
ancient indian mounds
where great sin was committed: (Joshua 6:26)
divination
worship of idols
human sacrifice, (1Kings 16:34)
over territorial spirits
is a commander
who orders other spirits
to come and go
spreading evil influence
across an area

against spiritual forces of wickedness
greek for "pneumatikos"
demonic spirits
sent from the air
by powers on earth
to demonize people, animals
parasitical in nature
like worms that live within a body
like leeches stuck onto a leg
both in and out
either
or

satan himself (Job 1:7)
walks the earth
coming from the air
may enter a human

war

as he did judas (Luke 22:3)
to destroy the work of God
so too do his demons
enter
to destroy God's work

spirits on earth—territorial
and demons—unclean spirits (Mark 1:23)
come to take territory (Daniel 10:20)
land and persons
claiming for satan

satan's copy of God's army
in the heavens
angel armies (2Kings 6:16-17)
sent to help believers
under the
Lord of hosts
Lord Jesus
on earth
sons and daughters of God
a spiritual army (Revelation 19:14)
separated into battalions
churches
within communities, cities,
prayer circles (Acts 12:5)

territory must be held by God
earth and people
churches and believers' homes
Godly territory
people
temples of Holy Spirit
to be kept cleansed of sin
and unclean spirits

the kingdom of light

when a church is closed
satan takes the territory
when a church expands
with satellite churches
God claims victory

as a human is born again
angels in heaven rejoice
it is God's victory (Luke 15:10)

a variety of spirits exist
which covet flesh*

the will of Jesus is to cast them out
as He did from mary magdelene (Mark 16:9)

spirits linger where lights flicker
without reason

the home must be anointed with oil
prayed over, cleansed, blessed
in the Name of Jesus
circling the property

*Mariades, Helena M., Strike the Target!, Xulon Press, 2010.

fleshly armies

the kingdom of darkness
fights against the ever increasing
kingdom of light
kingdom of God

darkness
moves at night
to church grounds
leaving curses
painted
at back corners
where no one seems to look

darkness
moves in disguise
entering church services
programs
to divide
to curse
to interrupt
to lead astray

darkness moves against
leadership
missionaries
evangelists
pastors
divorce, scandal, pride, porn
physical and verbal attacks
with weapons
with words
spiritual

miami
my Gospel team

came to santeria priest's door
the team plead,
warned him of hell and eternal fiery fire
pagan priest stood inside barred screen door
next to him on the concrete floor
santeria paraphernalia—chains, goat's skull, statue of a small boy
he stepped outside, but still stood guarding the doorway
after much time had passed,
he could not be unbound from satan's use
the priest grew up in santeria
deeply bound to cultural and demonic roots

satan's army in flesh
those rendered to his cause
who know his name, his demons
are as high-ranking pawns for his use:
priests and priestesses from the occult
voodoo
santeria
macumbe
yoruba
satanism
witches, warlocks
shamans

shape-shifters
those who take on in the spirit world
a different body
even an animal's
a spirit guide
a spirit animal
a power animal

astro-projection
coming as light into a dream
a tunnel filled with beautiful flowers
this is the demon-moved human spirit

war

coming through
to curse
to attack

spirit travel
to other locations
to curse churches
communities
Christians

as if a witch upon a broom

God's people on earth
are a mighty army
homemakers who spend the day in prayer
grandmothers on their knees
friends, brothers, sisters
cohorts, battalions, bands
banded together in protective prayer
over the sick
leaders
their church
their work
do not forsake the gathering of the faithful
for our good
a great shield of protection as requests are made known
necessary
vital

pastors, evangelists, missionaries
leaders who come against evil
to take back what satan has stolen
placing upon themselves by word
armor of God
helmet of salvation: protection of the mind
breastplate of righteousness
belt of truth: exposure of lies

sandals of the Gospel of peace
shield of faith: covers entire body
sword of the Spirit: Word of God (Ephesians 6:10-18)
cloak of zeal: God's desire at my back
garments of vengeance: the taking back of God's usurped territory
—casting out the enemy (Isaiah 59:17)

not all are called to go
challenging enemies
prayer walk,
but we are all called to pray
as a church
prayer from the faithful
helped bring peter out of prison

other pawns of satan
do not know his usage
oblivious
they are used unconsciously
just as those
who pray
for the death of Christians
islam

just as those who approach
doors
in God's name
an attack
jehovah's witnesses

just as those who believe
they are serving
their jesus
their god
but are deceived
ground troops
expendable

war

no person is beyond the reach (John 3:16)
and redemption of God
no matter how deep in the occult
nothing can separate us
from His love
He is our protection and our shield

isolation

lions come in darkness
to water's edge
where long trunks still suck
and drink

lions come in darkness
not in light
when an elephant sees less
and lion sees more
to isolate
attack together as a pride
a major kill

they jump up from behind
where tail descends
apart from sight
apart from tusks
running her until exhaustion
bringing her down together
feeding for a week

by day
the enemy heard me when
i prayed
Lord of the universe
take me and use me
for Your glory

for major attacks
the enemy moves against us
in our areas of blindness
mine was a generational curse of divination
father's
and generational iniquity of divination
mother's

war

i was a believer
alone without spiritual support
weak
having drunk only milk
ignorant of
curses
family iniquity
demonism's operations
and mental illness

the first spirit i knew
the spirit of fear
came as hysteria when very young
remaining until deliverance
it invited others in (Deuteronomy 28:28-29)
came as a serpent in the night (Job 4:13-15)

deaf and dumb spirit
draws a child to a pool, a pond
to drown her—as happened to me (Mark 9:21-23,25)
disassociation began here

weighed down with bitterness
a stronghold (James 3:14)

spirit of heaviness
descended with depression
begun very young (Romans 9:2 KJV)
led to thoughts of death (2Samuel 22:6)

spirit of divination: door opened many times
storybooks of witches, (Acts 16:16)
enacting fortune telling
horoscope watching

personal boundaries easily washed over (Deuteronomy 32:8)
evil entered my household (2Timothy 3:6)

to captivate me
beginning with the internet
led on by various impulses
into divination
the occult

i became a false prophet
writing and publishing online
under pen's name
secret sins, backsliding
i was self-deceived
double-minded
a spirit of error (1John 4:6)

spirit of infirmity
with mental illness
major depression (Acts 10:38)
worsened illness (Luke 13:11)

a lying spirit spoke
at the end
shocking me (Isaiah 28:15)

a spirit of death
spoke of suicide
deaths of others
encouraging me to plan to go away
as if on a long trip
mexico, canada, france
self-deception
hidden
its agenda
twisted into death (Proverbs 14:12)

a seducing spirit
drew me deeper and deeper
into darkness (1Timothy 4:1-2)

war

antichrist spirit
impressed an image
a devil on the cross (1John 4:3)

the enemy came at night
in dreams
in day
through meditation
strange visions
strange outside voices
strange people came into my life
all attacks,
major attacks occurred
at psychic readings
and at the end
when i
like an elephant was weakest
depleted of iron, serotonin, vitamins
spirit broken
mind splitting
exhausted from nights without sleep
hungry
from forced fastings

cracked
the enemy tried to kill me
through suicide
but i would not
or lock me up
but my husband would not

the enemy isolates for major kills
coming in with a band of demons (Psalm 78:49)
some to lie
the antichrist spirit
to turn one away from God—
music, the Word, the church,

each opens the door to another
until many feed off the kill
even a weak believer
for a time
until she's dead

a spirit of bondage held me
asked me for my will (Romans 8:15)
after he became aware
my husband said
"you were in prison"
yes
it was a prison
one i will never return to
one i would not assign my worst enemy to
it was hell on earth

He who the Son sets free is free indeed! (John 8:36)

the shield

roman military shields
were three-layered
decorated
as large as a door
curved
to cover a man
just below his eyes
above his helmet
to just above his feet
shod below with protective gear

paul calls believers
the church in ephesus
to take up the shield of faith
with which you'll be able
to extinguish
all
flaming arrows
of the evil one
satan (Ephesians 6:16)

roman soldiers did not work alone
but together
in bands, battalions, cohorts
when faced with hundreds
of flaming darts from the enemy
they locked shields together
completely covering themselves
protection

american culture is changing
the church is under attack
from many sides
her defense is the shield of faith
prayer of the faithful

locked together
in this way she may go forward
and hold her territory

to move forward
roman infantry moved into a wedge
pattern
called the pig's head
like a flock of geese flying in formation
interlocking shields
they would push into the enemy,
surrounded—
a square formed
at the center—
the commander
shields interlocked on every side
north
south
east
west

laying siege to an enemy stronghold
a tortoise formation was utilized
like a square
facing out
soldiers interlocked shields
those behind front lines
lifted shields to cover heads
interlocking
as a tortoise has a shell
inside
light-armed troops
protection

fiery darts bounce away

war

the church must keep her shield up
together
the Commander
Lord Jesus
at the center
Who directs the prayer
Who directs when and where
to move forward
into enemy territory
or to hold fast (Luke 19:13 KJV)

the sword

of the Spirit
which is the Word of God
must be spoken in prayer
in offence
against enemies

for the Word of God is alive
and active
sharper than any double-edged sword,
it penetrates even to dividing soul and spirit,
—removing demons,
spirits from the mind, the soul
to dividing joints and marrow
healing
it judges the thoughts and attitudes of the heart
what is within a man (Hebrews 4:12)

each day i walked
i passed a home
where squatters
drug dealers lived
blessing the home
with raised hand
"Lord please remove these drug dealers
and bring a Christian family"
a few months later
FBI
arrests
following
a new neighbor
whom i recognized from church
God's blessing

war

the santeria priest
asked   "who are you praying to?"
i pray to Jesus i answered

with a sword of the Word of God
he heard the truth
a few minutes later   "stop praying"
but i ignored him
i would obey no demon's voice

it is the Gospel which goes forward
and cannot be stopped
God's Word will not return void
but with fruit

the Word prayed
sees the return of a son from prison
another from drug addiction
it is the power of God
spoken through a believer
two months before the santeria priest's home
and watch the moving truck
drive him away

it is the power of God
spoken
before psychic stores
botanicas—occult shops
before businesses with names like
abyss, illuminati
as you pass places that rise up
against the knowledge of God
lift a hand
pray
"bless this place in the Name of Jesus Christ"
every time you pass by
and watch God begin

to work
to take back
what was stolen from Him

it is the power of God
spoken over me by a man of God
who ordered out dominating spirits
that refused to leave—
a frightening situation
like skin cancers on the body that speak
which cannot be cut off
that night
delivered

together

when racism's ugliness would not depart
believers came together
to march and pray
to stand
stand firm

leaders were taken out
but more moved forward
from ranks behind
just as roman soldiers did
holding shields
interlocked
over one another
persevering
until they had overcome
selma, alabama

when forgotten children
were left without a gift
shoeboxes were packed
by many thousands
reaching more than 100 countries
each day thousands of little ones
come to know the Lord
because of a gift
evangelism of the church
operation christmas child

a leader and prayer team
intercessors
in wales
prayed for england's protection
specific places

for God's intervention
soldiers were saved
world war 2
dunkirk

believers hemmed in
the middle east
existing 2,000 years
banded together
living side by side
survival
keeping churches alive
in memory of Him
nazareth

together in the upper room
the faithful
prayed
waiting
fire and power
fell from heaven
as tongues upon their heads
as tongues within their mouths
began to speak
of God
many heard
and were saved
the Word of God
a sword
prayer changes the world
jerusalem

candles
cut and carried
each hand

war

lifted high overhead
illuminating light
silent night's eve
each one
necessary to push out
shadows
darkness
a light, a hand, a voice
together
the light of the world
the church

death's door

at death
many see the dead
but the dead do not leave heaven
they call the dying to come
to deceive
demons in disguise

before Christ was risen
angels carried believers
to abraham's bosom (Luke 16:22)
paradise
to await arrival of Lord Jesus

fallen angels
demons
satan's copy
come for unbelievers
carrying their spirits and souls
to hell
the kingdom of darkness
to which they belong

for there is a choice
for kingdom loyalty (Colossians 1:13)
God's
or satan's

believers
children of the Light
sons and daughters of God
belong to Him

war

Lord Jesus receives us
He is resurrection power (Philippians 3:10)
our example
as Holy Spirit raised Lord Jesus
from the dead (Romans 1:4 NLT)
Holy Spirit seals our spirits
raising us to heaven at death

no surrender

this is war
spiritual earthly war
the fight continues until death
the High Commander
Lord Jesus
Lord of hosts—armies
calls for no surrender
stay the course (2Timothy 2:4-5)
fight the good fight (1Timothy 6:12)
hold your territory
your home, family, the place of work
God has given you
overcome
overcome evil with good (Romans 12:21)

i have been lied to
deceived into drunkenness
—someone drugged my drink
a roofie
the enemy came and laughed
accusing me of drunkenness
hurt
entangled
attacked in many ways
i have lived through nearly drowning
a major depression
a car crash
potential snake bite
a plane on fire nearly crashed
but with God's help
i too have overcome

even at death
the enemy may come
to take away those who could be saved

war

through false teaching
as i have seen with false ministers
in hospice

God has His own
the church
who goes out
and does good works
bringing men into the kingdom
before the end

the spirit of death
speaks to caretakers
through unbelievers
                      "don't help extend your loved one's life"
when they are old and ill
the spirit of death
speaks to the ill
                      "no one recovers from this"
do not surrender
not even at the end
church
pray for the dying
in the valley of the shadow of death
that Holy Spirit would protect
and see them safely through

Holy Spirit
guides into all truth (John 16:13)
it is God Who decides
when we will die
it is God Who exposes the evil
that we as the church might pray

it is God Who gives protection
through the end

casting out

identify the demon
the type
in your life, your child's, your spouse's
pray
"i come against
a spirit of _____
i bind it with the Blood of Jesus
rebuke it with the Name of Jesus
and cast it into the abyss
with the power of Lord Jesus
chained about the neck
until the day of judgment"

do you not know
that we will judge angels? (1 Corinthians 6:3)

the enemy
fearful of the abyss
begged Christ
not to be sent there (Luke 8:31)
send them!

break it

a son of believers
his dreams entered by satan
who ordered the child
                      "obey me, do not listen to your parents"
frightened him
psalm 91 prayed over and over
by mother
until he came to a teacher
who knew to break a curse
generational
voodoo
from haiti
God's power pulverized satan's right

ask forgiveness for sins
specific if known
of self
of fathers
4 generations back
10 generations into the future (Deuteronomy 23:2)
bind
cast out
enemies coming through the curse
and all demons under their authority
"i break the curse
in the Name of Jesus Christ"

after

casting out enemies
plead the Blood of Jesus over the person
seal open doors with the Blood
in prayer
never to be opened again
baptize him
with Holy Spirit
through laying on of hands
as in acts (Acts 8:16-18)
further protection
fullness of God's power
obedience

to God

i ran

when i could
i ran
like a gazelle from a leopard
to solace
and silence
to the place of aloneness
where thoughts distorted
could be assembled
by my subconscious
without direction
making sense to only me
fictionalized
truths altered to one's own fancy
dreams kept private
fantasy wished for
in psychosis
....becoming reality

when i could
i ran
until legs were chopped
and like a chicken's body
kept moving through air
keeping childhood's pace
with imagination leading
until body, mind, spirit
were halted
to face façades
to face demons of desire
like a sick gazelle caught
by her own body run amuck
the leopard came—to kill, to destroy
and so, i turned,
....to God

melt down

what's accumulated
equals
what's depleted
the two
yoked together
become
the storm of
mental illness
accompanied
by attacks of
demonization
creates
a meltdown

paper dolls

scissors clip, trim edges
fingers fold creases
carefully dressing
a paper figure
the two-sided flat persona
not fully developed
only one side
                    visible

named
she calls herself
the name

four
each one a new year
a mask of birth pains
worn over weakness
showing greatness's
façade

within,
the mind s e pa r a t es
the named dolls
yet remains whole
until divisiveness
determines detriment

each one
goes her own way
and the mind
like a ship
struck by a missile

fragments   apart
    and
            sinks

to God

spirit crushed
soul broken
      but not destroyed
major depression
leaves them sleep deprived

figures lying upon
dollar store carpet
each spilling tragedy's
tears

as voices echo,   ear   to   ear

in weakness
limbs torn,
coverings shredded
an exposé
and with them—
what lies
      beneath
the lies

long protected,
((((the inner self))))
thought to stand
its own guard
with paper—
but paper burns

within,
the inner self
reborn in God's image
waits patiently
four more years
enduring fear

Unbound

outwaiting running
until His peace
has settled
deep within

through fire
and torment from
                              hell

the inner self
known to Him—
what she will be,
has faced her greatest fear
and lived to tell
without false selves
her only guard—
the fruit of her lips,
JESUS

paranoia

anxiety spreads as contagion
infecting mind, emotion, body
and will
until all bow to the disease
paranoia
in dreams
nightmares
in wakefulness
as visions
until all of life
becomes
focused fear

struggle for self

where is the self?
covered in flesh, attached at birth
hurts heard, pinches pinned in mind's memory
nothing forgotten, buried deep within subconscious and brain's plasticity
becoming more than they should be
until i find myself in bathroom's corner
on knees, hands raised
to God, a quickened voice praying through
psychotic episode
there—that is self
gone are family, friends, love of flesh, wealth, the mind preparing to divide itself
when all else has been taken or given away, lost, withdrawn, even her name
her spirit emerges—and calls upon
GOD
who she is in Christ
this is the self

the house

the house of God
  shall be a temple
     of prayer
but you have
    made it
                    a den of thieves (Matthew 21:13)

do you not know
that your body
is a holy temple
a living sacrifice
    to God? (Romans 12:1)

satan comes before
the presence of the Lord
accusing the brethren
both day and night (Revelation 12:10)

the church
a building
where prayer
and worship meet,
also entering
demons (Job 1:6)
with those who carry them,
                  as sin (Luke 4:31-37)

some
their bodies
filled with Holy Spirit
unwittingly
allow the enemy entrance (Hosea 4:6)

as surely
as satan
stands before God
both demons within
and demons without
stand before Holy Spirit (1Kings 22:21; Zechariah 3:1)
in the life of
the believer

the place

life in a bell jar
sylvia plath's poetic despair
dying depths
in mind's deepest well
with no rope, no ladder
no way out,

his world, his own
of government agents
and secret deception
trailed john nash
as grand delusions
hallucinations
brilliant
even beautiful
circling round and round
again

i too know this place
its loneliness
where all come in
and none go out
the subconscious spilling over
into the conscious
voices
hallucinations
paranoia
of enemies

Unbound

a classic psychotic episode
found at the bottom
of a major depression
where the mind begins
to crash
divide
come unglued

a place of terror,
entrapment
a place
which though hidden
has an **Exit Door**
lit in red letters
even the lintel,
even the trim
narrow
and difficult to enter
but very very real
as sure as my paper
as sure as my pen

to bring relief
to bring an end
never to repeat again

"I am the door; if anyone enters through Me, he will be saved,
and will go in and out and find pasture."
(John 10:9)

the precipice
(first published in the anthology *I Have a Name*, CTU Pub 2017)

her side woundless, his wounded for transgression. sin known and unknown, passed from father to children, giving them hope and many false starts, which begin when track's gun speaks and shortly ends when it repeats. drugs, like vitamins, a handful thrown back with a coffee chaser: (remembering dad, remembering the end of his life, remembering cancer) "he cannot care for himself, he cannot care for himself." that's OCD—the repetition of talk which does not end, but causes torment end to end; a perfect circle—hoolihooped in the head; an earworm which plays over, over, over like a broken record, like a return button—a return to what is reality, what is real, what is inside the head, mimicking itself, a silent mime unseen, but deafly heard. its roar deafening as niagara's falls.
the precipice of the fall, descent into psychotic symbiosis.

what happened

my mind fractured
as a lamb thrown from stormy sky
hits, breaks in pieces
upon sea's waves
other names
personas
the sentence of death within me
upon me
affecting my children

i should have died
or worse
awoken to find myself
institutionalized
forgotten

few return as i did
afflicted, forlonly afflicted
but not destroyed (2Corinthians 4:8)
preserved by the Lamb
the Blood
His grace

to God

the prophet

i swallowed God
and made Him my own
a spiritual presence
emanating from
                my voice,   my mind
and i became more than what
i could become
                            crying in the wilderness
a daughter
pious in all her ways
leaving luggage
leaving love unpicked upon   the tree

the pull

as a crawling baby is drawn to a pool
what pulled me in to darkness
DEEP,
some call it: the occult
one thing: sin
like Eve, i wanted to know more, more of what is forbidden to
know, to see, to experience
darkness DEEP is subtle,
  one step down into the water—first the toes, the feet, the ankles
        until i found myself walking under water
each thought won to the side of evil, evil dressed in light
as an angel, as Jesus, even as Holy Spirit speaking as God
my weaknesses in mind, in body known by satan
and like a passenger jet hitting a twin tower
i was used
and drowning under water—
a prayer prayed on commanded knees, bowed before a beast
beside a bed;
a beast who mimicked God in power, God in anger, God as an
abuser who "loved" only me;
who directed impressions—some stills, some motion pictures,
"infusions" of spirit too—
sensations upon head and mind
four square—like a game, they played with me—ball bounced
between
like cats do a mouse
demanding duty, love, obedience of commands
sent to psychics who listen to familiar spirits
and there received a spirit through the laying on of hands
and i submitted, i submitted, i submitted
as jonah submitted to God, so too did i—
an immature believer
because i believed the enemy was God

tabebuia tree

middle-aged trees bloom
lemon blossoms littering
sidewalks
of my life
leading to the beach
of yesterday
my youth, my decline
into major depression
where i sat and waved away
darkness
to the feet of God
for judgment

the blooms
half shed
like tears from eyes
numbed by medication
half yet clinging
to the Branch (Zechariah 3:8)
of hope,
of continued life

seeds planted in the past of
"don't look back"
into the past
when children scampered
in autumn's wind
kite string in hand
before blooms' bud
before the shoot became
the branch
the tree now grown
cannot go back
to become the sapling
greening with vibrancy:

a child swept up in
mother's arms
memory lost
between mother and daughter
the memory lost
of what never was

to God

the trial

three days in a wilderness
devoid of food
without sleep
scratching my back
his attacks in visions
repeating
he came
as God
as a test
to try my knowledge
to try my body, my mind, my spirit

on the third night
demons surrounded
i bowed before Jesus
asserting that they too bow
i bowed before Jesus
before who he was
unmasked himself
a demon
who claimed to be satan himself

after the trial

i ran,
at 2AM my hand clenched
upon my husband's
so tightly
he awoke
enemy exposed
the attack continued
but Holy Spirit spoke
"tell your husband"
mind unsure,
i wavered
enemy answering   "no, he will kill you"
and then,
i spoke
and peace between us
began

voices

voices echo
repeating
themselves
redundant
memories
impressions
over and over
never ending
never muted
but covered
by surf's roar
upon beach's sand
where i lie
face covered
attempting to ignore
trying to understand
the torment
never knowing
it was
a major depression

who am i?

i can make a list
of who i am
the branches
      salt of the earth
           light of the world
they laughed
though
back then
the voices heckling
which woke me
in the night

                        "light of the world...."
                  "she does not even know
                      that she is the light
                          of the world...."

        "You are the light of the world.
     A city set on a hill cannot be hidden."
             (Matthew 5:14)

pulled out

first strike: a call to God

the time of fullness,
of understanding,
of belief had not yet come
i did not know who i was
nor what needed to be cleansed
within

until
demonized, depressed, ready for destruction
breaking into mental pieces
spiritual pieces
only then did i comprehend
danger
evil demanding death
which is counted
the wages of sin, (Romans 6:23)
in fear
i bowed my knees, heart, mind to Christ
the only One
Who could defend me
sobbing soulish sobs
"help me Jesus!
help me!"

pulled out

first nights

my husband's left arm
around me
his right hand
on my head
switched sides on new sheets
beneath my pillow
a wood-covered
Bible

i dreaded sleep—
nights filled
with dreamy violence—
attacks and voices
through doors unlatched
speaking to
my mind
my ears
closer—
closer even than
my husband
fear sought a stranglehold
upon my mind
i prayed
and the voice answered:

                                        "He doesn't hear you"

deceiver

after enemy outed
i lived in fretful fear
afraid of aloneness
voices followed

i lay upon the couch
exhausted
swallowed by
post traumatic stress
results of attacks,
repeating a lie
"they are not real"
"they are not real"
"they are not real"
it slithered out
rising beside my face, my ear
it lay across my chest

                                                              "i am not real?"

a threatening
terrifying voice
from outside
print cannot describe
it left
deceiving the deceiver

so simple

so simple, they say
to order them
out
in the Name
and yes   they go
but will return

to fight
for territory

still considered
weak
in the night

unmasked
when prayer is dear

                                  "shh….go to sleep"

"Jesus is Lord"

                                    "He is yours,
                                 but He is not mine"

through waterless places
                       traveling
only to return (Luke 11:24)
to fight with pain
like a bullet
to the head
and coldness
to the body
through doors not shut
to fight with lies

                                     'i …..love……satan'
"Jesus!"
a fight i could not fight
alone
the fight Holy Spirit helped

me win (Zechariah 4:6)

so simple, they say
but these do not know
nor understand
the great weakness of man
the frailty of mind
the necessity of Christ
and the Word
of the mouth (Proverbs 18:21)
when we are sifted (Luke 22:31)
like flour
by demon's hand (Job 1:7-12)

last glance

highlander humming,
attentively waiting
at a stopping red light
skin prickling with sweat
rear reflection
showing space, time,

between then and now
here and there
kinetic energy
traveling
a speeder

'she needs to slow down.
we're at a red light here'
eyes turn forward
hands clenching
10 and 2,
right foot
firmly pushing brake

'i'm just overanxious'
neck tilted up
for last glance back
'1, 2…'

a demon
a hellish hurtling
bashing into my backend

a rear attack
back and neck
snap forward,
the crash—a trial, a test
a living dummy

Unbound

hitting the black BMW ahead,
and back again
seat broken
engine squealing
smoke burning
panic,
unbuckling
checking for life,
demon departed, (Mark 5:1-13)
the grandma dead.

territory

i was territory
they had rights to me, they claimed
to my life—given my will
(but one cannot truly give it)
squatters' rights at best

                                    "you've gone back to Jesus"
i 'd never left Him, nor He, me
but there are those, like me, who are deceived
eyes opened by Jesus
no longer usable in darkness,
like the mafia, they chose to kill me

that day
that two-second moment
a perceived presence upon the car's driver
her life overcome to hit my own
blood's ruptured aorta caused her death

but by God's grace
i lived
i lived to tell of the greatness
of my Lord and Savior Jesus Christ
my testimony ends
as it began
God has always protected me

    "His faithfulness is a shield and bulwark." (Psalm 91:4b)

the basement

there is a great divide between
the mountain of consciousness
and its shadow
the subconscious
a valley with a rift so deep—
to keep separation,
there darkness
is rolled tight
within subconscious crevices
like a havana cigar,
a parasitical stronghold (Ezekiel 30:15)
clinging to access—begun
too young

a figure
a young boy
his mouth opened wide
outside door's glass
he speaks, yells—becomes hysterical
until the door slides open
by my hand
in the night
without pause—
he enters
the basement
of the subconscious

each year his friends
the silly, the busy, the sick and infirm
follow in where he
has entered

finally, four
strong muscle men
armed with anger and brutality

pulled out

are deliberately chosen
and they too enter
descending from the conscious
from kitchen stairs

crowded and crammed (Mark 5:9)
territorial fights ensue
pushing thoughts
from back to front
subconscious to the conscious
waking up their host
to Truth (John 16:13)

and i can take no more

by the Spirit
i order—
"get out!"

scurrying feet
exit the glass slider
as i remain glaring
until every last one
has stripped dead works
from life's walls
and vanished
into darkness's night

and all that remains
upon basement's walls—
the work of the Cross
hangs alone

the bridge

together we thrust our feet
forward,
step by labored step
side by side
up the bridge of brow's sweat
above dolphin fin current
and wayward jellyfish
until we stand
breathless
above the river
barrier between
mainland and island
the bridge
between reality and fantasy
where i had
charmed sunbathers
who knew no otherness

with
encouraging words
he motions how

raising my right arm,
as if on pitcher's mound
i hurl it
silver spinning switchblade
end over end
stories downward
splashing
sinking
beneath river's chopped surface

pulled out

never to be reached for
again
a weighty burden sinking
washed of my blood
by the Blood
set free
by Truth

> "So if the Son makes you free, you will be free indeed."
> (John 8:36)

the counselor

in my time of need
how did i find her?
God did
He led ....me...................
as the Shepherd (John 10:14)

the book on the nightstand
the doctor-author who answered
his home phone
his assistant
whose wife
is a Biblical counselor
through whom
He works
to save
the single ewe sheep
lost and
crying in the wilderness
"help me God!"

i asked her
"never give up on me"
she answered
"i won't
and neither will God"

> "For I am convinced that neither death nor life,
> neither angels nor demons,
> neither the present nor the future,
> nor any powers,
> neither height nor depth,
> nor anything else in all creation,
> will be able to separate us
> from the love of God that is in Christ Jesus our Lord."
> (Romans 8:38-39 NIV)

the heart

the sharp edge slices through
peel and flesh
of the darkish avocado
firm, yet soft
palatable
and catches on the pit
tip held fast within the heart

my heart
heavy and thickened with turmoil
i stand at dock's end
where water laps night's sand
my voice and mind
together sing
"it is well…
it is well…
with my soul.…"

firmly, i press downward
core divided
halved by steel and strength

with every last bit
i cling to my Anchor (Hebrews 6:19)
                                        "you've gone back to Jesus"

falling open
exposed
the heart,
white, tender, young
the flesh,
ripened
cores' cover

my soul
now shattered—
a lamb broken in pieces
and sinking
beneath shadows
which attack
like beasts of prey

peel pulled back
avocado's meat sliced
and laid neatly upon
the dish,
the heart to be
tossed as garbage
and sifted as flour
or saved to the uttermost

my Anchor

holds firmly
upon river's bed
and nothing can
and nothing will
separate me
from His love

the husband

each night he turned
his head, his side
upon the bed,
upon his pillow
where tears leaked silently
with silent calls for help
to his God
night after night
until Holy Spirit
urged an hour of prayer
in nazareth (Luke 4:34)
at mary's well
where the Savior grew
into a man

he bent his head
and once again
lifted his voice
"Lord, if You are real....
i don't care about the money,
just bring my wife back"

the osprey

the osprey's eyes
like mine
are double-lidded
with goggle-like membranes:
he dives into waters
and sees with eyes open—
but paper-thin, covered
his claws sink into fish flesh

mom's are double-lidded too
tinted pink as roses
to see the world
on fair's tilt-a-wheel
i learned from her
to push away fear
with hearty laughter

my world became
the deep maroon
of lovely mature roses
where no fear could show
no anger flourish
and happiness chose
to be a façade of choice

and as the osprey
watches his prey—
so i began to look
for what was
in what was not
through maroon-hued glasses
long outgrown but yet perched upon my nose

bad looked good
perverseness twisted truth (Isaiah 19:14 NKJV)
with lies

"what is the truth?"
i finally asked
and when lifelong glammed glasses
were removed
He revealed the lies
the evil
the bad
and cleared my vision
with His own

> "So Jesus was saying to those Jews who had believed Him,
> 'If you continue in My word,
> then you are truly disciples of Mine;
> and you will know the truth,
> and the truth will make you free.' " (John 8:31-32)

finding self

a key

one memory is a key
which unlocks others
a step
       down
              decaying
                      wooden
                              stairs
each unsteady, unbalanced by experience
where mother's trunk clasps her locket dear
secrets kept which held the truth
leaving me in ignorance
to disassociate
separation of self from self
the loneliest place to reminisce
years and years of separateness

memories

stick like gorilla glue
impressed upon the mind
interpreted through
innocence

yet each one
pulled off mind's wall
prompted by Holy Spirit
is examined
made right
with counselor's help
of what really was
and what really is
helping me to stay present
connected
in touch with God and man

bone-tired

when i am bone-tired i neither sink nor swim
but bow my head, raise my hands
and say,
i cannot serve two masters:
either parents or God
either husband or God
either self or God
two masters—
—the first always requiring Old Testamentish goodness,
becoming obedient, and hiding self
—the second himself, like him, of him,
becoming him and losing self
—the third requiring absolute perfection, boosted fleshly pride,
weakness
works wound within heart's stride
which only festered deeper wounds
no, i am bone-tired, even of self

strength

He has given me strength
each day
to overcome
a lack of boundaries
to say "no"
and preserve myself
His living sacrifice
His boundaries
His will
i can only serve the One
He Who loves me

finding self

each day

    each day   a journey

                  begun in pain
              stretching of limbs
                and muscles
                  and mind

                    jumpstarted
                      after
                hallucinations
              major depression

                     each day
              awaking to dread
            of beginning again
         when life's littleness
            holds the body
                      down
                      high
            with chin held
                  just above
                    waters

                     each day
              thoughts looking
                  backward
                  in horror
                 of what is
                 what was
and what could h a v e   b   e   e   n
                  but isn't

    each day   a journey

stuck in time
four years became
a perpetual two,
at 50

i once was 35

new days

each day made new
as we meet together
in prayer
in Word
You speak to me
encouraging my life
as a lily (Luke 12:27)
providing all that i need
my days
aglow
abundant bursts
of heart-flower hues

false shame

i hurt myself with shame;
out of my memory
i hear my mother clomping up the steps
shouting, "where is that brat?!!"
and i am 23
a university graduate
a teacher
a responsible adult
why does it matter?

when i turned away
following myself, following God
instead of her directives—

a black sheep who walked to the beat
of a different drummer
a perfectionist dutifully trying to be good
—or else
this is my rant of memories held too tightly
choking up on the bat before
striking out
but still trying
trying so hard to gain
even win
parental appreciation
approval
why do i need parental approval?

looking deep within the prattle
i see the shame which came about unnecessarily
because i wasn't deemed good enough
wasn't wanted enough
nor loved enough

that empty place within
filled itself
with shame
why is it false shame feels like shame all the same?

despised

He too
knew the rejection of men
despised by those He loved (Isaiah 53:3)
despised by those He came
to save
the walk of Jesus
good enough for God (1Corinthians 1:28)

finding self

instead

instead of sadness
    see the beauty
    in what is left

at middle age
trousers stubbornly unrolled
eyes turned yet toward Michelangelo

remembering the good in him and her
and those who hurt me
trading
truncating memories in a subway turnstile
                      "cuh thunk, cuh thunk, cuh thunk"
fare paid in full
for the metrocard—memories colored ugly, colored hurtful

each ticket a departure from stops long passed by:
    seen only as history
    until coming to line's end

all things

all things
....diversions into the occult
....childhood
....mental breakdown
....attacks
....physical illness
all things
work together for good

for me
because i love the Lord
and He has called me according
to His purpose (Romans 8:28)

lost time

i have lost 50 years
of life
because i didn't
know
who i was

the days were evil
stealing
from me
through depression's
wrong thinking
precious choices

misconstrued
and lost
He protected me
even from myself
and sought to show me
what needed
to be peeled away
what needed to be
washed (Ephesians 5:26)

peace must be apprehended
as if a thief
leaving through the window
in the dead of night
peace must be made
as two generals aboard a ship
enemies
come to understandings

i hang up my running shoes
and see the future needs
only shoes for walking

step by step
across forever
what was lost
is much less
than what was found
forever (John 3:16)

one word

one word and then
another
each   taken   in
absorbed
as salt upon oil
removing stain
removing darkness
which familiarity clings to
the fear of failure
the knowing of self

the wall

the wall, wide and white
clean   pure   false
self-imposed
security, as for a prison
until a hand
appears
to write words
which determine
who, what, when, why
how
predetermined (Psalm 135:6)

finding self

pony

He Who is true Who is no malicious master
gave free rein to a prairie-running pony
her life held tightly in His grasp
but gave her freedom none the less

bones tiring, she slows to trot
and yet He lets her pace her own
protecting her from slough and mud
night's horse thieves, wolves with gunny sacks
her life held tightly in His grasp

longing for approval
she stops, head drooping in submission
lips languishing for liquid
sides heaving
rasped breathing pitiful
her inner voice only, crying
"not my will, but thine" (Luke 22:42)

His grasp upon the reins, remains
gives His little pony rest, a drink
then turns her with His gentle hand
back upon the path which He has planned
a plan of peace, of purpose, of place
His way—safe, and best

rocks

my life has been backed
to cliff's edge
at a word
lever pushed
load engaged
the extension
                        lifts the dumping bed
a full load of rocks
all sizes—
boulders, stones
              and pebbles

p
    o
        u
            r
                o
                    u
                        t

gravity pulls them forward
faster f
      a
        ll
       i
          n
            g

into the DEEP
                r   ne
            a   i
              v
                                  boulders, stones
                                          and pebbles

finding self

into the pit
of my stomach

my mind has been
jarred
back to reality

of who i really am

sin

his wings tiring
the insect comes to rest on window's sill
behind plate glass
a prison wall, invisible, he remains trapped
indoors
Lord, you have searched me and know me (Psalm 139:23)

i am the young woman baptized—
the sin i saw—

                                                      gone

the sin i did not see
                      remaining

as a curse
as filth upon my
                                                     back

secretly, ignorantly passed from parents to me
even to the fourth generation (Exodus 20:5)
father to child, father to child

spiritual blindness— like a window which will not open
(2Corinthians 4:3-4)

teachable eyes have seen, have heard
and do as was done before them
upon them

spiritual blindness—allowing me to be guided by evil,
both evil men and the enemy

unbroken dominoes falling before given a chance
to stand

when God's time comes, prayer opens her mouth
and prays
"not my will but Thine be done"

finding self

and again
"Lord, if there is anything of the old man remaining in me,
reveal it, and cleanse it." (Galatians 6:15)

when God's time comes,
what is hidden was revealed
the old man stripped away
one curse
one layer
one promise at a time
outer skin peels —   discarded, burned, and given up for dead

the dig

"who are you?"

to know who i am
must i remember
what is best left
lost
buried beneath
the sea of forgetfulness
or pick it up
two hands of the bride
carrying
a bouquet of
forget-me-nots

like old potatoes
left beneath earth's
bare field
harvest years now past
i return
with trowel in hand
upon covered knees
to dig

treasure
each one
blighted
reminders of childhood
famine
a time of craving
words
unheard

with neck bent forward
tears speckle dirt
kid gloves

finding self

gently place each
lifeless tuber
into a golden bowl
filled with
the incense of prayer (Revelation 5:8)

rising
i brush earth
from white clothing
shake my sandals
of dust
and continue
walking

the door

the door faces forward
not behind
not hidden
is not locked

the frame and lintel
    brushed with living Blood (Exodus 12:7)

the door opens
when the knob is turned
    from the inside
    at persistent knocking
    in fear, illness, despair or love

the Door is the Way (John 10:7)
    to life
    to freedom
    to healing

the Door is the Hope
    of dreams fulfilled
    life renewed
    truth in life after death

the Door is only One
    not many
    not in magic
    not in dreams, strange voices or images
    and does not exist in subconscious' realm

finding self

the Door is **Jesus**,
    the Son of God
   Who saves us
         from ourselves
         from lies, trickery, deceit
         from enemies, curses, and even (Galatians 3:13)
         from death
   Who saves us
                to the uttermost
            from behind the gates of hell
Who saves us

  when we were children
     when we are oblivious
         when we were sick
            and even when we yet sin

grape vine

His love is like a grape vine
Whose root remains growing

                    20 feet

                      underground

                        into the soul

                        the heart

                        the mind

                        and

                        He

                        can
                        not

                        be

                        pulled

                        out

                  as He saved me, so too can He save
                                          you

finding self

"I am the vine, you are the branches;
he who abides in Me and I in him,
he bears much fruit,
for apart from Me you can do nothing." (John 15:5)

cycling down

green cross dream

—January 7, 2012
she sleeps
gentle dreamer
upon sheets
of pine
new needles
abed
a pillow
a dream:
glowing against night's dark sky
neon green
immense
bulging forth
with life

she looks
she sees
she remembers
great green cross
glowing with living light
printed down center's beam
J
E
H
O
V
A
H

R
A
P
H
A

bold black blocks
Hebrew
His Name
"I AM the Lord
Who heals you" (Exodus 15:26 NIV)
healing from head
to sole
to soul
a promise made
a promise kept

legible
across the bottom
a baseboard
upon the foundation
Jesus Christ
a verse
a direction
a plan
Jer 33:3
"call to Me
and I will
answer you
and I will tell you
great and mighty
things
which you do not
know"
a promise made
a promise kept

cycling down

night's vision
from God
Who establishes
His church true
as green as the cross
is red
upon His disciple
she sleeps
gentle dreamer
guarded by
the Lord

privacy

the sounds of privacy
shout longingly
inside window's gaze
two chairs, both occupied by self and soul
Spirit between the two, a table bare
where we three daily meet
to speak with saliva-dry untongued words,
wet ink

each offering addressed with prayer

pen upon closed lips
allowing what will, will recall
deep thinking
scattered thoughts, ideas of oddly color
pushing as a grocery cart
basket filling with a recipe
registered at once

switch, vary, edify, omit
as rubic's cube
turned left and right, forward, back
until a pattern shifts, sets
as jello in a copper mold
never a cross word exchanged
until we three agree
click save
and print
privacy—
        thoughts made sound

selah

an interlude, a time of waiting
between the writing, the publishing
this the time of finalization, introspection
can i do it?
will i do it?
deep within
"i can"
"i will"

launched out into the deep
my boat, filled with nets
of words
13
a baker's dozen
12 for the Lord
but all are His

He rides with me
through narrow channels
endless miles of ocean darkness
at the front,
He points the way
revealing with His light
what remains hiding in shadows
schemes from hell (Job 3:8)
to drain believer blood
too early

transitions

words are transitions
which cannot fly
her boundaries firm upon a page
letters, each tied with type
black on white
left to right
left to write
a little more
                                            a little less

words are transitions
like lightning synapses
through gray matter a message sent
embedded at gene's bequest
recalling a place, a time, a whiff
a climb
a little more,
                                            a little less

words are transitions
from child to adult
each year more gathered and gleaned
as a hen scratches her yard for seed
ingested, used, garbage pooped out
retaining the best
a little more,
                                            a little less

cycling down

words are transitions
which flow as color
creating painter's canvas in several strokes
shading subtle gradation sunlight to gray
quietly receding
loudly bellowing
imperceptible change both out and in
a little more,
                                      a little less

words are transitions
which transcend
breaking boundaries
mind to Mind
through Spirit
through God
through time
a little more
                                      a little less

"Take the helmet of salvation and the sword of the Spirit, which is the Word of God." (Ephesians 6:17)

He takes

what was riddled with prints
of princes
flown out of hell

burn it

diary of darkness
fallen rotten fruit
                gathered by day
              from whispered words
                demon direction
                visions impressed
            as if playing roulette
          sorcery, magic, mistakes

burn it

fallen rotten fruit
                gathered by night
              from dreams of deceit
          entered by familiar spirits
        open doors to the subconscious
           entered by human spirits
                astro projection
      demon-assisted spirit movement
            to rape, deceive, destroy
            voices heard in darkness
                    scriptural
                      cold
                    laughing

burn it

cluttered, collected, kept
turned into writings
published as a prophet
though false
theme: end days

                                          He takes it all

cycling down

        the writing gift
knowledge of the tree of good and evil
        and gives her a book
            empty
    and instructs her to write
     things both old and new
        God's poet
giving her His strong support
       in every way

all things made new
redeemed by the Blood of Jesus

        to save many
      crush oppressors
     to glorify the Son
        Lord Jesus

the meat

"but solid food is for the mature,
who because of practice have their senses trained
to discern good and evil" (Hebrews 5:14)

those who drink milk are of two kinds
guzzlers and sippers
guzzlers cannot get enough
reading much
to fill them quickly

sippers take a little here
another sip there
steadily drinking

milk is for infants
holding them,
feeding them
oracles of God
beginning principles (Hebrews 5:12-13)

but there is another who partakes of the Word
one who is accustomed to the Word of righteousness
the mature
who has practiced what he has read
having trained his senses to discern good and evil

he eats the meat of the Word
solid food
stabbed with a fork
cut with the knife
piece by piece
each bite slowly chewed
until ready to be swallowed

each Word precise
meaningful
necessary
for understanding;
the Word of God cannot
be broken (John 10:35)
it is life-giving food

the covenant: a delusion

                              "offenses will come"

the car pulled forward
left wheels aligned
with conveyor
gear moved to neutral
hands dropped from the wheel

the tunnel swallowed the car
machines dove forward
spraying
turning themselves
against windshield
doors
windows
the world obliterated
by soap, bubbles, water
                        but the radio continued
                          voice filled Scripture

light shone at the end
strong winds blew away residue
seamless drying

this is my life
the tunnel
the machines
attacks upon me, my work
but i will remain safe within His will
hands off the wheel
in neutral
while He moves me slowly through
day after day
            His voice yet filling my ears with His Word

"prepare for war"

                                                                          opposition
physical, spiritual, mental
on earth and in the heavens
as humans, as demons
written and spoken

"offenses will come"

                       "covenant with Me and I will keep you safe"
Lord, i will do this work
and if You allow this prayer of a righteous one,
i petition You to include these things as part of the covenant:

the united states be Bible-based, bordered, boundaried
immigration shut to all except believers
that You would provide
transportation, lodging, food, medical and mental health care,
and work to immigrant believers

crush the oppressors and save the children

as i preach the Word of Jesus,
signs and wonders to follow in a way that has not been seen
since the Lord walked the earth 2,000 years ago
dead raised
new limbs grown
cancers removed
autistic children and adults healed and delivered
sicknesses that have no cure—healed

i pray great prayers Lord because You are the Lord of the universe
the only One to cry out to: there is no other
i ask these things not for myself
but for Your glory and so that the world would know that what i
speak for You is Truth
Your Truth

my husband and children protected

please provide for my family and me as You have promised

reveal to me the deep things of the Word
hidden
encrypted
that will save many

i pray the whole world would hear Your Truth

i promise to the best of my ability, though i am weak in every way:

Kelly Jadon
                                          your humble servant
                                                Kelly Jadon
                                            August 3, 2016

the snake lay dead upon the street
desire of delusion
grandeur that takes the mind to a place
far future
trumped once again by coping mechanisms
to endure
there is no queen, no chief judge, no expert
of last days
no last days' prophet, no nazarite calling
there will be no kingdom on earth today
paranoia's purposes run amok
like oil wells lapping over my feet
sucking seductively

cycling down

until i prayed purify me
that i may be a living conduit of Your power
and "anything God"

He began to reveal truth
and set me free

standing: satan uses me

standing in the gap, as the queen,
in songs of praise,
words of thanksgiving
in repentance of self
in repentance back to the root,
binding, casting out demons blocking the way
asking for mercy
what He gives me for the mercy seat
using His Name
pleading the Blood
invoking His Spirit
claiming His prophetic promises
keeping still
there is no queen
the battle is His

now they know
                                                      "i hate you"

prayer interruption attempt
"rebuke it"
directive from Holy Spirit
"i bind this speaking enemy—wings, eyes, mouth
with the Blood of Jesus
i rebuke it with the Name of Jesus
i cast it out into the abyss with the power of Lord Jesus
to be held with chains everlasting
about the neck
until the day of judgment"

another
dark, shadowy pressuring presence
beside me
evil
thinking to scare me
"i shall fear no evil"

"rebuke it"
directive from Holy Spirit
bind
rebuke
cast out

"is this discernment too much for you?"
"no Lord, i need to have spiritual discernment"

now they know

as the youth trespassing upon my property
moves away and out of my field of vision
so too does the enemy

discernment
a gift of God
the weapon of our warfare
divine power to demolish strongholds
where demons reside
now they know

new covenant

the door of the ark closed
world left behind
my father's footsteps finished
his house ended
                              the Lord will carry me
                    lead me forward
            into the promised land
a place i do not know
have never seen
as a mother, a wife, a substitute teacher
when He calls
i must go
                                to pull the children out,
                              hold them back
warning
speaking truth
blessing
                          even baptizing with Holy Spirit
breaking the curses
    spoken, generational, in the body, doors to the mind
prayer
prevention, teaching the Word of God
petition
deliverance
"in the Name of Jesus!"
    language
a spoken Word ministry
to children brought to God
by parents
    anything
i prayed
enlarge my territory Lord
with Your hand upon me
keeping me from harm

cycling down

a work never done before
call me out upon the waters Lord
as peter
came to You alone   i am not my own
                                    i lay me down

free the children Lord   there is no life
of cancer   apart from You
curses
depression, mental illness
autism
all sorts of maladies
their bread
each a stone in the kingdom
                the city
                    New Jerusalem
                      You build
Lord—You have filled me with knowledge, wisdom, discernment, and Your power
to do the good works You have planned for me
i watch for You to lead Holy Spirit

committed to You

transition

transition

a time to lessen
more of Him
complete and utter dependence
upon God as Father
closening
laying down self-will
—the natural
inclinations: adventure, excitement, care-taking, job hunting
daily dying to self

it is as a hallway
palacially lengthy
a corridor
connecting one place to another
through which i walk
praising
the Son of God

strategic

the day came
for such a purpose
in my life
eukairos
—everything comes together
the morning Word
watching
waiting
it arrived as a text
"kelly, you are a woman of God"
Holy Spirit message
through obedient vessel

transition

lowly

last
serving all
lead me Lord
as i have prayed for Your answer
"what will i do?"
minister
comfort, comfort
comfort others as you have been comforted

quiet strength

repentance
rest
quietness
trust
with all my heart
without understanding
why move me from there to here?
acknowledging Him in every way
asking Him to intervene
when rejected, despised, disrespected
He makes straight the path
Defender
Answerer

those who honor Me
I will honor
those who despise Me
will be disgraced (1Sam 2:30)

word curse

came as a blessing
with a hug, a smile
through kabbalah
a doctor
in return
i took his hand
blessing him in the Name
of Jesus

                                        "i believe in Jesus"

"i know you do"

but the Lord is only a man to him
even the demons believe
and tremble (James 2:19)

"i break that curse
in the Name of Jesus"
i left that doctor
never to return again

revenge not

as attacks
rise up as a lioness
to pounce upon prey
so must i remain as deaf
and mute (Ps 83:13)
pay no mind
plot no revenge
preventing my own sin
dealing with men of base spirits
who hand out evil for good
remaining with You Lord
faith, prayer
less stress
to answer for me
Judge

transition

promised

"for you are about to cross the Jordan
to go in to possess the land
which the Lord your God is giving you,
and you shall possess it and live in it" (Deuteronomy 11:31)

what has been promised?

a place of reckoning
recognizing
admonition of sins
gently
antibiotic
for festering disease
within the body
slowly killing
its life

first look into my own life
cast out any grudges
make apologies
forgive each remembered hurt

clean me Lord

burdens lifted

what i gave to Him
He took
transformed them
placed them elsewhere
burdens
that i might not be hindered
halted
stopped
that i might rejoice
in His goodness
and serve Him daily
at His will

ready to use my own name

birthing

as a mother carries within her womb
a warm well-loved lamb
yet unborn, unnamed, unsaid
so i have carried my story
close to my heart
birthing it
for a purpose
as suicide rates climb
divorce descends
the world winds awry
—that others would see the Light
instead of declaring demolition
shooters shooting others
instead of suicide
enough said
—that others would not be tazed to death
mistakened a criminal menace
shot instead
—that those in institutions come to know
saving power
which goes within
even the mind, the heart, the soul
—that many could renew marriage vows
reconnect with children, mothers, fathers, friends
—that family could understand
the nonexistence of selfishness
the prison of self and satan
and secrets kept for generations
because of stigma
because of sin
because of ignorance
—that truth of spiritual darkness be exposed
as it battles against God's children
both day and night

"Take no part in the worthless deeds of evil and darkness; instead, expose them." (Ephesians 5:11)

the trigger

tapping on my psyche
putting into motion
of another escape
the trigger:
stress

mental, emotional
even physical
until burnt out as a hollowed house
i crash
learning more of self
leaving more of old self

finally
admitting
i do still have flesh of the mind
lingering rememberings
habits since infancy
how i disappeared as a child
mental illness
a weakness
a thorn which pricks deeply (2Corinthians 12:7)

but i am His
His weak thing
He holds me up as i am weak

ready to use my own name

misunderstood

selflessly
i gave myself
as if a sacrifice
to a gun-gleaming
mouth to mouth
bullet chambered gun,
my wrist slit slightly
in defiance
against who i thought God was
in a war
where darkness sought control
against self
and dark voices threatened

selflessly
i believed that i was worthless
nothing, not necessary
better without me
became isolated
alone

selflessly
i believed if i did not go
i would die of cancer
nuclear fallout would destroy
my family
i would be all alone

i believed
no way out of mental madness
melancholia
existed
which came as demonic control
demons playing on mental weakness
keeping me ignorant of my mental state

so subjective
so chained
i could not see the truth

death appeared as quietness
ending of entrapment
within mind's mind-trap
boxed in a labyrinth

no money
no fame
no forced laughter
no loving friend
nor family
all affected
a human experience
misunderstood

you wish to die?

hey you!
yes you
the one who wishes to die
you aren't the only one
i did too
to escape reality
myself
my misery
to escape lies,
delusional fantasies found false
hallucinations which crawled upon my body
and a mind that wouldn't stop

to you who wishes to die
i know your pain
like a knife in heart's heart
lack of love
running, pushing away love
before it crucifies you again
i know your hurts
emotional, mental, physical
your neglect and abuse
i know how it feels to be stigmatized
called "crazy"
"delusional"
pushed away
pushed aside

to you who wishes to die
i have been where you are now
a child
a marriage rocked upon ragged shores
my children aghast
left thinking
"i don't want to be like mama"

do i blame them?
no
i want no one to suffer as i have

to you who wishes to die
before you cut the wrist
deliberately overdose
tie the noose
cock the gun
jump
roll over niagara's falls
or run your car off bridge's brow
count the cost:
children left floundering
lost
unable to fulfill yet folded dreams
a father, a mother, husband, wife
who will carry to the grave
"my fault"
who in turn
turn the mouth to mouth
testing trigger's strength
a double memorial

do not believe

                          "this is no way to live"
                          "i'll never get better"
                          "there's no way out"

i testify
there is
with God—
all things are possible
He is the Door
which opens to help
to healing
to guidance
even

ready to use my own name

the right medication

do not give up
upon yourself
you are not alone
cry out
"help me Jesus!"
and begin to see the way
out of living dead
to living
really living
life

seek **JESUS** with all your heart
you will find
the way out
and become
unbound (Daniel 3:25 NIV)

> "Jesus said, "With people it is impossible,
> but not with God;
> for all things are possible with God." (Mark 10:27)

About the Author

Kelly Jadon is a writer and poet. She also publishes an online column, "Hometown Heroes." Her previous book is, *To Taste the Oil: The Flavor of Life in the Middle East* (2014), a book of poetry bringing alive the forgotten Christians of the Middle East. Her poetry has been published in various literary journals both online and in print.

Kelly was educated at Spring Arbor University, the University of South Florida, the University of Iowa's International Writing Program, Laubach Literacy, Toastmasters International and Christian Leaders Institute. Kelly Jadon is an Ordained Minister, holding a Diploma in Christian Leadership. She resides in South Florida with her husband of more than 30 years. Together, they attend Morningside Church in Port St. Lucie, Florida.

Email: kfjadon@gmail.com
More information: www.KellyJadon.com

Made in the USA
Columbia, SC
23 June 2021